Bible Stories Revisited

Discover Your Story in the
Gospel of Luke
and the
Acts of the Apostles

MACRINA SCOTT, O.S.F.

ST. ANTHONY MESSENGER PRESS

Cincinnati, Ohio

Nihil obstat: Reverend Timothy P. Schehr
                     Hilarion Kistner, O.F.M.

Imprimi potest: Reverend Fred Link, O.F.M.
                     Provincial

Imprimatur: Most Reverend Carl K. Moeddel
                     Vicar General and Auxiliary Bishop
                     Archdiocese of Cincinnati
                     September 2, 2004

The *nihil obstat* and *imprimatur* are a declaration that a book or pamphlet is considered to be free from doctrinal or moral error. It is not implied that those who have granted the *nihil obstat* and *imprimatur* agree with the contents, opinions or statements expressed.

Scripture citations are taken from the *New Revised Standard Version Bible*, copyright ©1989 by the Division of Christian Education of the National Council of Churches of Christ in the U.S.A., and used by permission.

Cover and book design by Constance Wolfer
Electronic format and pagination by Mark Sullivan

Library of Congress Cataloging-in-Publication Data

Scott, Macrina.
  Bible stories revisited : discover your story in the Gospel of Luke and
the Acts of the Apostles / Macrina Scott.
     p. cm.
  Includes bibliographical references.
  ISBN 0-86716-425-5 (alk. paper)
  1. Bible stories, English–N.T. Luke. 2. Bible stories, English–N.T.
Acts. I. Title.
  BS2595.55.S35 2004
  226.4'09505–dc22

ISBN 0-86716-425-5
Copyright ©2004, Macrina Scott, O.S.F.
All rights reserved.
Published by St. Anthony Messenger Press
Printed in the U.S.A.
04 05 06 07 08 5 4 3 2 1

Prayer Before Bible Study

O Loving God, you plant your word
like seed in our hearts.
Send your Holy Spirit to nourish
this precious seed
and make it bear fruit
for your glory.
This we ask through Jesus
your Word Made Flesh.
Amen

Acknowledgments

THIS BOOK WAS BEGUN DUE TO THE ENCOURAGEMENT of the many graduates of the Denver Catholic Biblical School who used my earlier book, *Bible Stories Revisited: Finding Your Story in the Old Testament*, either individually or in leading small discussion groups.

It was tested on various groups over the last few years, and those group members and facilitators both encouraged me and suggested valuable improvements.

The entire manuscript was edited and vastly improved by my devoted friends Judy Sassetti and Kathy McGovern. Lisa Biedenbach of St. Anthony Messenger Press provided the support without which the book would never have been written, as well as final editing.

Contents

Introduction

MANY INDIVIDUALS AND SMALL GROUPS who used my earlier book, *Bible Stories Revisited: Finding Your Story in the Old Testament,* have asked that I provide a similar guide for reflection and sharing about the New Testament. This book is a response to their enthusiasm. I have selected the two volumes by Luke—the Gospel of Luke and the Acts of the Apostles—as they provide the longest unified narrative in the New Testament and studying them together throws much new light on both.

Many of us learned Bible stories as children. When we revisit them later in life we bring a rich treasure of life experience that gives a depth and meaning to the stories far beyond what we could have imagined as children. At the same time, the biblical stories help us to appreciate and share stories from our own lives.

I was motivated to write this and my earlier book by my excitement over one of the new phenomena of our times: large numbers of persons who live many healthy years after completing their responsibilities to their children and their careers. These "extra" years, so rare in the past, now provide new opportunities for a large part of our population. These include extraordinary opportunities for spiritual growth. Retired people are free to pursue the inner journey in a way that was not possible while they were burdened with the demands of the earlier phases of life. However, because the pressures of the previous years often prevented them from acquiring the tools needed for inner work, this rich opportunity may be lost. This book aims to provide one of these tools: the ability to use the Scripture as a way of reflecting on one's life.

What This Book Includes

— Stories from the New Testament, with reflections based on modern scholarship and on the experience of the author. The reflections aim to prime the pump of each participants' own life experience.

— Questions to enable the reader to reflect on the stories in the light of her or his own experience. These are not questions that have right or wrong answers. It has been said that the way human beings learn is by taking two stories and placing them one on top of the other. When we place our story on top of the biblical story we learn more about both.

— Suggestions of other passages of Scripture that will throw additional light on the passages just read. These make good reading between group sessions.

What This Book Does Not Include

— Clear, simple answers to life's problems. In Scripture, God gives us stories to help us reflect on life issues, not clear-cut answers.

— Academic research about who wrote these stories and when they were written, the cultural background of the stories, and why translations sometimes differ. These questions require a much bigger book than the present one.

Who Can Use This Book

This book is suitable for persons with or without biblical background. It bypasses the issues dealt with in academic biblical study to focus on actualization of the biblical stories.

It is particularly suitable for persons of any age who are willing to reflect on the aging process. There are individuals of all ages who choose to avoid reflection on aging. They may not be comfortable with this book.

Ways to Use This Book

In a group, ideally of four to eight persons. The questions provide an opportunity for sharing of different life experiences, which enriches all participants and brings the stories to life even for those who have not personally experienced anything like what happened in a particular story. This could be a group of friends, a parish group, a group in a senior center, or a bridge club that wants to do something different for a while.

The chapter can be read aloud if there are good readers in the group. One person should read the commentary and another the Scripture quotations, in order to emphasize the distinction between the two. It is important for readers to prepare, as the quality of the reading can make or break the session. A group may choose to have several readers for a Scripture passage, each taking a different part. If the members prefer, or if there are not skilled readers available, the meeting can begin with quiet time during which each one reads the chapter silently.

The opening prayer (which is found at the beginning of the book) is best read by all together. Some groups may want to add prayers for particular intentions or a hymn, such as "Come Holy Ghost."

It is important to name a facilitator. The role of the facilitator is not to teach but to encourage all participants to share their life experience as it relates to the biblical story. If the facilitator has biblical training he or she may also answer any questions members raise about the scriptural story, but this should not take more than a few minutes. "Hints for Facilitators" can be found on the next page.

Each session will probably take about 75 minutes: 35 for reading aloud, and 40 for discussion and prayer. Some groups may want a longer discussion, but it is important to set the schedule ahead and stick to it.

As a couple. Two friends or a married couple can read and discuss together, in much the same way as a group.

Alone. The book can simply be read through, but will have greater value if the reader pauses to reflect on the questions or uses them for journaling.

Miscellaneous Items

Each chapter is able to stand alone. So, a group might use a single chapter as part of a meeting, or do a series of four, six, eight, twelve or twenty-four. There is a natural division between the first twelve chapters, which deal with the Gospel of Luke, and the second twelve, which deal with the Acts of the Apostles. The first three chapters are particularly suitable for Advent and Christmas; Chapters Ten, Eleven and Twelve are particularly suitable in preparation for Holy Week and Easter.

The author is indebted to authors and teachers of Scripture who have cast light on God's word for her over the past fifty years. Their insights have become so much part of her that she can no longer trace her ideas to their sources, nor does the format of this book permit it.

The translation used here is the New Revised Standard Version. It uses small capitals for the word LORD whenever this translates the Hebrew proper name for God.

Introducing Luke

LUKE IS PROBABLY THE ONLY AUTHOR of a biblical book who was not a Jew. He is also the only Gospel writer to write a second volume showing how the story of Jesus continues in the story of the church. Today it is common to study his two volumes, the Gospel of Luke and the Acts of the Apostles, together. By doing this we can see how he shows many parallels between Jesus, Peter, and Paul. Luke wants us to see the continuity in God's work. What Jesus began is continued in the church.

Like every biblical writer, Luke highlights material that illustrates themes that are particularly meaningful to him, and which he wants his readers to appreciate.

Perhaps because, as a Gentile, he was a minority person in the church of his time, Luke's main emphasis was that Jesus comes as savior for all people, with a special emphasis on those who are disadvantaged in some way.

Conspicuous among the disadvantaged in any culture are the materially poor. Luke stresses that Jesus came as a poor man and showed special love for the poor. Since some of Luke's readers were rich, he stresses that they should use their wealth to help the poor.

Others who were marginalized by his society are also important for Jesus: the hated tax collectors, prostitutes, Samaritans and Gentiles. The sick were also marginalized, either because of their physical condition or because their affliction made them ritually unclean, that is, forbidden to take part in the life of the Jewish community.

Women were highly disadvantaged in Jesus' society, and Luke likes to emphasize how Jesus not only healed them, but also invited them to become his followers. Widows, generally the poorest among women, come in for special attention.

So Luke gives us a picture of Jesus who comes to save all, especially those in most need of salvation. He does all this in the context of a journey. Even in his childhood, Jesus makes two journeys to Jerusalem. As an adult, he spends a large part of the Gospel on his way to Jerusalem to his death and Resurrection. The story of the infant church, on the other hand, begins in Jerusalem and gradually makes its way to Rome. This theme of journey gives a unique dynamism to Luke's two volumes. Everything is in movement toward a goal set by God.

This dynamism comes from the Holy Spirit. Luke alone tells of Pentecost, and of the action of the Spirit in the life of the early church. He also shows the Spirit as very active in the life of Jesus, especially in its beginnings. Since the Spirit brings joy, joy is the dominant tone of Luke's writing.

The Spirit also inspires prayer. Luke tells us more than any Gospel about the prayer of Jesus, and his instructions on prayer. It also gives us several prayers we find nowhere else: Mary's song of praise, Zechariah's hymn, the angels' song at Jesus' birth, and the prayer of Simeon. The kind of prayer most important to Luke is the prayer of praise. He often closes a miracle story by remarking that all present were amazed or praised God.

Where did Luke get the information from which to compose his Gospel? He makes no claim to be an eyewitness of the life of Jesus. He tells us, "Since many have undertaken to set down an orderly account of the events that have been fulfilled among us, just as they were handed on to us by those who from the beginning were eyewitnesses and servants of the word, I too decided, after investigating everything carefully from the very first, to write an orderly account..." (Luke 1:1-3). It seems that one of the sources Luke investigated was the Gospel of Mark. His special insights come out in the way he changed some of the stories he took from Mark, and in the stories he found in other sources and added to Mark.

One way to get a feel for Luke's special approach is to read the stories that are found only in his Gospel:

Stories Unique to Luke

Luke 7:11-17: The Widow's Son at Nain

Luke 9:52-56: Rejection by the Samaritans

Luke 10:29-37: The Good Samaritan

Luke 10:38-42: Martha and Mary

Luke 11:5-8: The Friend Who Comes at Midnight

Luke 12:16-21: The Rich Fool

Luke 13:10-17: The Healing of the Woman Bent Over

Luke 14:1-6: Healing of the Man with Dropsy

Luke 15:8-32: The Lost Coin and the Lost Son

Luke 16:1-9: The Unjust Steward

Luke 16:19-31: The Rich Man and Lazarus

Luke 17:11-19: The Ten Lepers

Luke 18:1-8: The Unjust Judge

Luke 18:9-14: The Pharisee and the Publican

Luke 19:1-10: Zacchaeus

Luke 19:41-44: Jesus Weeps Over Jerusalem

Luke 24:13-35: Emmaus

Key Places in the Gospel of Luke

CHAPTER ONE

John and Jesus

Annunciation to Zechariah

IN THE FIRST TWO CHAPTERS OF HIS GOSPEL, Luke draws a parallel between Jesus and John the Baptist. John's birth is announced, he is born, circumcised, named, and grows up. Jesus' birth is announced, he is born, circumcised, named, and grows up. Luke wants us to notice the similarities, but also the differences. John is preparing the way for Jesus. Jesus is greater than John.

We have to know about the parents of John the Baptist in order to appreciate what Luke wants to tell us about the mother of Jesus. The parents of John the Baptist were elderly and highly respectable people, of the revered priestly tribe, and outstanding for their observance of the innumerable rules that governed the daily lives of pious Jews. But their lives were tragic because they had no child. And Elizabeth was beyond the age of childbearing.

> In the days of King Herod of Judea, there was a priest named Zechariah, who belonged to the priestly order of Abijah. His wife was a descendant of Aaron, and her name was Elizabeth. Both of them were righteous before God, living blamelessly according to all the commandments and regulations of the Lord. But they had no children, because Elizabeth was barren, and both were getting on in years.

Luke 1:5-7

God sent an angel to announce to Zechariah that, despite the human impossibility, they were to have a child. As befitted an honorable priest, he received the angelic message in the holiest place in the Jewish world, the sanctuary of the temple in Jerusalem. It was the day when he had been chosen for the great privilege of entering the sanctuary to burn incense. His reaction was that of most biblical characters visited by angels. He was afraid. Even the most pious and respectable of us don't really expect to see angels, and it can be unsettling.

The angel's response is also one often heard in Scripture. "Do not be afraid." The angel then promises Zechariah the birth of a son who will play an extraordinary role in God's plan. This child will prepare the people for the Lord by turning the hearts of parents toward their children. It seems as if God cannot come until reconciliation has happened between the generations, and that the first move toward reconciliation must come from the parents.

Then the angel suggests that the son will be a Nazirite. That is, a person who could drink neither wine nor strong drink because of a special dedication to God (Numbers 6:1–21).

> Once when Zechariah was serving as priest before God and his section was on duty, he was chosen by lot, according to the custom of the priesthood, to enter the sanctuary of the Lord and offer incense. Now at the time of the incense offering, the whole assembly of the people was praying outside. Then there appeared to him an angel of the Lord, standing at the right side of the altar of incense. When Zechariah saw him, he was terrified; and fear overwhelmed him. But the angel said to him, "Do not be afraid, Zechariah, for your prayer has been heard. Your wife Elizabeth will bear you a son, and you will name him John. You will have joy and gladness, and many will rejoice at his birth, for he will be great in the sight of the Lord. He must never drink wine or strong drink; even before his birth he will be filled with the Holy Spirit. He will turn many of the people of Israel to the Lord their God. With the spirit and power of Elijah he will go before him, to turn the hearts of parents to their children, and the disobedient to the wisdom of the righteous, to make ready a people prepared for the Lord."

Luke 1:8-17

———

The old man's response was not enthusiastic. (Perhaps God would have done better to have sent the angel to Elizabeth.) True, when he was young, he had prayed ardently for a child, but that time of life was over, and he no longer had any such hopes. He may not have felt up to the responsibilities of raising a son at this point in his life. He objects that this is not possible because of his age and his wife's. We can imagine the angel Gabriel pulling himself up to his full height as he overwhelms the old man with his authority, then announces that he will be punished for his disbelief by becoming unable to speak. The priest who no longer expects God to act in his life is not worthy to speak to the people. When Zechariah returned to the people who were waiting outside, he was mute.

Zechariah said to the angel, "How will I know that this is so? For I am an old man, and my wife is getting on in years." The angel replied, "I am Gabriel. I stand in the presence of God, and I have been sent to speak to you and to bring you this good news. But now, because you did not believe my words, which will be fulfilled in their time, you will become mute, unable to speak, until the day these things occur."

Meanwhile the people were waiting for Zechariah, and wondered at his delay in the sanctuary. When he did come out, he could not speak to them, and they realized that he had seen a vision in the sanctuary. He kept motioning to them and remained unable to speak. When his time of service was ended, he went to his home.

Luke 1:18-23

———

Annunciation to Mary

All this has been to prepare us for the story of the annunciation of the birth of Jesus, which is parallel to the annunciation of the birth of John the Baptist, yet contrasted to it. Again Luke begins by introducing the characters and the setting of the scene. The same angel, Gabriel, comes to a very different person: not an elderly and respectable man of the priestly family, but a young engaged girl. In a society where neither youth nor women were respected, this was a big comedown compared to Gabriel's mission to Zechariah.

The contrast is emphasized by the location. Gabriel found the priest Zechariah in the most revered place in the Jewish world, the sanctuary of the Jerusalem temple. He finds Mary in Nazareth, a tiny village of so little significance that it is never mentioned in the Old Testament, in the writings of the historian Josephus, or in the Jewish Talmud. Later, when Nathaniel is told that Jesus is the Messiah he will quickly dismiss the idea on the grounds that nothing of significance could come from such a place as Nazareth.

Nazareth today is a busy place, full of pilgrims from all over the earth. At its center are two large churches. The space beneath these churches was the whole of Nazareth in Jesus' time. It is quite an experience to enter the very large and beautiful church of the Annunciation, then climb beneath it to the remains of first-century Nazareth. Archeological work has uncovered the crude caves in which about twenty families lived, and remnants of the simple room that was built on to the front of each cave. One cave even has its oven clearly visible. Since there is no sign of ovens in the other caves, probably each woman brought her bread to be baked by her more fortunate neighbor who had an oven.

We are not told that Mary, like Elizabeth and Zechariah, came from a respected family, or that she was known for her observance of the religious rules of the Jews. We are told that she was a virgin, as was taken for granted for an unmarried woman in the highly moral Jewish society. But this was not an honor, simply a way of saying that she had not yet arrived at the normal role of a woman as wife and mother. No one at the time realized that the Messiah would be born of a virgin.

Even her name hardly suggests an extraordinary person, as it was one of the most common names for women at the time. One of the difficulties of New Testament study is keeping all the Marys straight.

> In the sixth month the angel Gabriel was sent by God to a town in Galilee called Nazareth, to a virgin engaged to a man whose name was Joseph, of the house of David. The virgin's name was Mary.

> *Luke 1:26-27*

Gabriel greets Mary in the words that have echoed through the centuries in the "Hail Mary." Like Zechariah, she was troubled at this unexpected visit. The angel responded, as he had to Zechariah and many others, "Do not be afraid." As he had told Zechariah, he tells her she is to have a son, what the son's name is to be, and what his role will be in God's plan. This son is not to prepare the way for someone else, but to rule forever on the throne of David.

If Zechariah had reason to say that what the angel promised was impossible because of his age, Mary had better reason to question how this could happen to her, a virgin. The angel replied in an extraordinary way, "The Holy Spirit will come upon you, and the power of the Most High will overshadow you." This child will be son of God and of Mary, but will have no human father. Nothing in her whole religious heritage had prepared Mary for this. Gabriel tried to help by giving her as a sign the other miraculous birth that was to take place, that of John, and reminding her that *nothing* is impossible for God.

Unlike Zechariah, Mary comes to faith. She is the first disciple, the first person to hear the good news about Jesus and accept it. She is also the first person to risk everything for Jesus. Luke does not point this out, but from Matthew's Gospel we know that this unplanned pregnancy put the young woman in a small village where moral standards were high into a very difficult predicament. Mary accepted her role without knowing how she could avoid being stoned as an adulteress. She was open to the strange ways of God.

> And he came to her and said, "Greetings, favored one! The Lord is with you." But she was much perplexed by his words and pondered what sort of greeting this might be. The angel said to her, "Do not be afraid, Mary, for you have found favor with God. And now, you will conceive in your womb and bear a son, and you will name him Jesus. He will be great, and will be called the Son of the Most High, and the Lord God will give to him the throne of his ancestor David. He will reign over the house of Jacob forever, and of his kingdom there will be no end." Mary said to the angel, "How can this be, since I am a virgin?" The angel said to her, "The Holy Spirit will come upon you, and the power of the Most High will overshadow you; therefore the child to be born will be holy; he will be called Son of God. And now, your relative Elizabeth in her old age has also conceived a son; and this is the sixth month for her who was said to be barren. For nothing will be impossible with God." Then Mary said, "Here am I, the servant of the Lord; let it be with me according to your word." Then the angel departed from her.

Luke 1:28-38

Two Mothers Meet

Luke has carefully structured his first two chapters as parallel stories about John the Baptist and Jesus. Only in this scene of Mary's visit to Elizabeth do the two meet.

The angel has given Mary as a sign that her elderly relative Elizabeth was also pregnant. One impossible thing was to be a sign of another. The young woman, astonished and frightened by her pregnancy, takes a trip of ninety miles over rough, hilly terrain, to visit Elizabeth.

This is an encounter between two strong women, women of different generations whose lives were tied together in the same mysterious work of God. The old woman and the young need each other. Elizabeth needs Mary's young energy, and her help around the house.

Mary needs a mentor, someone who can help her to understand what was happening to her. Young people need a mature family member or friend to whom they can come in times of personal crisis, knowing they will be accepted no matter what. They do not need to be told what to do as much as they need to be held lovingly while they work out their problems.

When Mary entered Elizabeth's home and greeted her, the child in Elizabeth's womb leapt for joy. Joy is a favorite theme of Luke. He shows that Jesus brought joy into the world even before his birth.

Elizabeth is filled with the Holy Spirit, another favorite theme of Luke's. At this moment of the quickening of the miraculous child in her womb, she might well have been filled with her own story. Instead she focuses on her young visitor. She cries out loud the words that have been echoed down the centuries in the "Hail Mary." "Blessed are you among women, and blessed is the fruit of your womb!" Elizabeth can affirm without envy the privilege of the young woman whose place in salvation history will be greater than her own. She even seems to contrast Mary's faith with her own husband's lack of faith. "Blessed is she who believed."

In those days Mary set out and went with haste to a Judean town in the hill country, where she entered the house of Zechariah and greeted Elizabeth. When Elizabeth heard Mary's greeting, the child leaped in her womb. And Elizabeth was filled with the Holy Spirit and exclaimed with a loud cry, "Blessed are you among women, and blessed is the fruit of your womb. And why has this happened to me, that the mother of my Lord comes to me? For as soon as I heard the sound of your greeting, the child in my womb leaped for joy. And blessed is she who believed that there would be a fulfillment of what was spoken to her by the Lord."

Luke 1:39-45

So far, the story has told us what was happening in Mary's life. Now for the first time we find out how Mary felt about it all. In the presence of this supportive kinswoman she breaks out into her Magnificat, the song of praise that has inspired innumerable musical settings and which is still used daily in the church's evening prayer.

Mary has heard Elizabeth's greeting, "Blessed are you among women." Now she expands that by proclaiming, very accurately, "All generations will call me blessed." But this is no expression of pride. Pride is claiming for ourselves what is God's gift. Mary is very clear that it is the Lord who has done great things for her. To refuse to recognize what God does in us is not humility, but lack of gratitude. Mary proclaims her greatness, yet she is the humblest of women. This is her prayer:

> And Mary said,
> "My soul magnifies the Lord,
>   and my spirit rejoices in God my Savior,
> for he has looked with favor on the lowliness of his
>   servant.
>   Surely, from now on all generations will call me
>   blessed;
> for the Mighty One has done great things for me,
>   and holy is his name.

Luke 1:46-49

Mary sees her own marvelous pregnancy as part of a bigger picture: of God's whole plan. So her prayer broadens beyond her own experience, to all past and future generations. She sees God's plan much as Hannah did: as a total reversal of human ideas. God will bring down the mighty and raise up the lowly; fill the hungry with good things and send the rich away empty. This theme of reversal is a favorite one of Luke's. He has Mary introduce it here. Later he, and only he, will give us the story of the dramatic reversal of Lazarus and Dives. His version of the Beatitudes, too, will be built on the theme of reversal.

The Magnificat is a song to cast fear into the hearts of the powerful of this world. It is a favorite of revolutionaries, those who want to turn existing social structures upside down. In fact, some Latin American dictators have forbidden it to be prayed aloud! This poor peasant girl speaks for the oppressed and underprivileged of all ages. Mary's prayer continues:

> His mercy is for those who fear him
>> from generation to generation.
> He has shown strength with his arm;
>> he has scattered the proud in the thoughts of
>>> their hearts.
> He has brought down the powerful from their
>> thrones,
>> and lifted up the lowly;
> he has filled the hungry with good things,
>> and sent the rich away empty.
> He has helped his servant Israel,
>> in remembrance of his mercy,
> according to the promise he made to our
>> ancestors,
>> to Abraham and to his descendants forever."

And Mary remained with her about three months and then returned to her home.

Luke 1:50-56

—m—

Now we return to John's story. The promise made to
Zechariah in the temple was fulfilled. The angel had
promised the old Zechariah not only that he and his wife
would have a son, but also that many would rejoice at his
birth. Here is the fulfillment of the promise.

> Now the time came for Elizabeth to give birth, and she
> bore a son. Her neighbors and relatives heard that the Lord
> had shown his great mercy to her, and they rejoiced with her.

Luke 1:57-58

According to the instructions God gave to Abraham, the child
was circumcised on the eighth day. It was customary to give
the child a name at that time. In the Bible, the one who gives
a name is the owner, the one in charge of the one named. It
is God, through the angel, who gave John's name. Elizabeth
and Zechariah only acknowledge the name already given.
With that acknowledgment, Zechariah is forgiven his lack of
faith in the angel's message, and is able to speak again.

> On the eighth day they came to circumcise the child,
> and they were going to name him Zechariah after his
> father. But his mother said, "No; he is to be called John."
> They said to her, "None of your relatives has this name."
> Then they began motioning to his father to find out what
> name he wanted to give him. He asked for a writing tablet
> and wrote, "His name is John." And all of them were
> amazed. Immediately his mouth was opened and his
> tongue freed, and he began to speak, praising God. Fear
> came over all their neighbors, and all these things were
> talked about throughout the entire hill country of Judea.
> All who heard them pondered them and said, "What then
> will this child become?" For, indeed, the hand of the Lord
> was with him.

Luke 1:59-66

Questions for Reflection

1. How do you think you would react if an angel came to you?

2. What people do you know who, like Elizabeth and Zechariah, found themselves with a child to raise when they were no longer young? What blessings and problems come with such a situation?

3. God sent Gabriel as a messenger to Zechariah and Mary. Whom has God sent to you as a messenger?

4. What do you think Mary and Elizabeth talked about in the three months they spent together?

5. At a time of crisis in her life, Mary went to her elderly relative Elizabeth. When have you known of a young adult who went to one of the older generation at a time of crisis?

6. Mary said, "God has brought down the powerful from their thrones, and lifted up the lowly." When have you seen this happen?

Suggestions for Further Reading

Luke, chapters 1 and 2

1 Samuel 1, 2, 3, 4 (Luke shows Jesus' beginnings as similar to Samuel's.)

CHAPTER TWO

The Children Grow

The Birth of Jesus

LUKE CONTINUES TO PARALLEL THE STORIES of John and Jesus. John's birth is announced, he is born, circumcised, named. The same happens to Jesus, but his birth is introduced more solemnly by reference to the Emperor Augustus. There were no B.C. or A.D. dates as yet! It had been enough to say of John that he was born when Herod was king of the Jews. Luke wants us to know that Jesus will be important for the entire Roman Empire, the world that he knew, so he tells us he was born in the reign of the Emperor Augustus.

He also wants to show that Jesus came from humble people, who obeyed the whims of those in power even though it meant the ordeal of giving birth to their child in a strange place. Other Jews had been known to rebel when subjected to a census, but not Joseph and Mary. Mary had prophesied in her Magnificat that the mighty would be put down and the lowly raised up, but she waited for God's time for this to happen.

The mighty Augustus, who had never heard of Mary or Joseph, was actually being used by God. The parents of Jesus lived in Nazareth in the northern part of the Holy Land. But the Messiah was to be born in Bethlehem, in the south. Bethlehem was the city where David had been born, and Luke wants to remind us that Jesus was legally part of the family of David. Joseph acknowledged him as his son legally even though Jesus was not his son biologically. According to Jewish law, this made Jesus a descendant of David.

Bethlehem must have been crowded at the time of the census, because the only place Joseph could find for Mary to give birth to her child was a place usually used by animals. Perhaps this was the season when the animals were in the fields with their shepherds, so their usual place was empty. I hesitate to call it a stable because that brings up images of a red wooden barn-like building. Wood was very precious in the Holy Land, and caves were plentiful, so animals were usually kept in caves. The manger from which the animals ate was usually also of stone. For Luke, the importance of the manger was that the child who was laid there would be food for the world.

> In those days a decree went out from Emperor Augustus that all the world should be registered. This was the first registration and was taken while Quirinius was governor of Syria. All went to their own towns to be registered. Joseph also went from the town of Nazareth in Galilee to Judea, to the city of David called Bethlehem, because he was descended from the house and family of David. He went to be registered with Mary, to whom he was engaged and who was expecting a child. While they were there, the time came for her to deliver her child. And she gave birth to her firstborn son and wrapped him in bands of cloth, and laid him in a manger, because there was no place for them in the inn.

Luke 2:1-7

Luke tells us simply that the neighbors of Elizabeth and Zechariah rejoiced at the birth of John. He gives a fuller description of the reaction to the birth of Jesus. He paints a third annunciation scene, this time to shepherds. Shepherds were not very respectable people at the time of Jesus. They were dirty, and could not possibly follow all the complicated kosher regulations about washings and so forth. They were also suspected of being dishonest. Their testimony was not acceptable in a law court. Luke wants to show us from the beginning that Jesus comes especially for the poor and less-than-respectable.

When the shepherds see the angel of the Lord they are terrified, and the angel has to begin, as angels always do, by telling them, "Fear not." The angel goes on to assure them that he brings good news that is to be a cause of joy for *all* the people, even shepherds. The news is that a savior has just been born in Bethlehem. As a sign, they are told that the child is wrapped in bands of cloth—the old translations said "swaddling clothes"—and lying in a manger. It is an interesting sign. The swaddling clothes show that this baby was prepared for with love and the usual clothing of infants was ready for him. But lying in a place meant for feeding animals shows that his parents are so poor they cannot provide a decent house for his birth.

The messenger-angel is then joined by a host of singing-angels who praise God in the words we still use in the Gloria at Mass. Only Luke gives us these poetic prayers: the Magnificat, the Gloria, the Benedictus of Zechariah, and the *Nunc Dimittis* of Simeon, all of which are part of the official prayer of the church.

> In that region there were shepherds living in the fields, keeping watch over their flock by night. Then an angel of the Lord stood before them, and the glory of the Lord shone around them, and they were terrified. But the angel said to them, "Do not be afraid; for see—I am bringing you good news of great joy for all the people: to you is born this day in the city of David a Savior, who is the Messiah, the Lord. This will be a sign for you: you will find a child wrapped in bands of cloth and lying in a manger." And suddenly there was with the angel a multitude of the heavenly host, praising God and saying, "Glory to God in the highest heaven, and on earth peace among those whom he favors!"

> *Luke 2:8-14*

These not-very-respectable shepherds came straight to the tiny village of Bethlehem, where it was not difficult to locate the child who had been born that night and was now lying in a manger. They told their story of the angelic choir, and everyone was amazed. But only of Mary are we told that she "kept all these things, reflecting on them in her heart." Other translations say that she "pondered" these things, or "treasured them in her heart." Here Luke tells us some very important things about Mary. Privileged though she was, she did not consider it beneath her to learn from shepherds. And she did not assume that she understood God's ways; she pondered all that had happened to her. Luke does not tell us so, but I think that pondering must have continued throughout her life, especially in her old age, when she could look back on the whole marvel of her son's life and death and Resurrection. Mary's vocation was not to preach or work miracles or organize the church; it was to be present with Jesus and to reflect in her heart on all that concerned him. Let's listen as the shepherds' story continues.

> When the angels went away from them to heaven, the shepherds said to one another, "Let us go, then, to Bethlehem to see this thing that has taken place, which the Lord has made known to us." So they went in haste and found Mary and Joseph, and the infant lying in the manger. When they saw this, they made known the message that had been told them about this child. All who heard it were amazed by what had been told them by the shepherds. And Mary kept all these things, reflecting on them in her heart. Then the shepherds returned, glorifying and praising God for all they had heard and seen, just as it had been told to them.

Luke 2:15-20

When eight days had passed, Jesus was circumcised according to the instructions given to his ancestor Abraham. Sometimes we forget that Jesus was not a Christian. He was a Jew, properly incorporated into the Jewish community by circumcision. Like every Jewish mother, Mary was distressed by the pain caused her infant son, and at the same time proud to see him made part of her people. Later, he would establish a new covenant, open to people of all races. But Luke wants us to be aware that the new covenant was established by one who was himself rooted in the ancient covenant with Abraham.

Then, like his cousin John, he was given the name that had been determined by the angel. God had plans for this infant.

> After eight days had passed, it was time to circumcise the child; and he was called Jesus, the name given by the angel before he was conceived in the womb.

Luke 2:21

Journey to the Temple

Luke, who is so careful to show that Jesus' parents observed every detail of the Jewish law, is not a Jew himself, and he does not seem to understand the two separate rituals that were performed when Mary and Joseph brought the Child Jesus to the Temple. One was the presenting of the firstborn son in memory of the sparing of the Israelite firstborn in the Exodus. The other was a ritual of purification of the mother after childbirth. This had nothing to do with dirt or with sin; Jews never thought of sex and childbearing within marriage as sinful. It was not the child itself but the bleeding after birth that made the woman unclean. This "uncleanness" simply meant that one could not participate in liturgical worship. It was removed by a ritual bath.

I have seen the excavations in the temple area in Jerusalem that have uncovered a large number of *mikvot,* or pools for ritual immersion, just outside the temple entrance. Thousands of pilgrims might need this purification before entering the temple on a feast day, and each needed a tiny private space in which to strip and immerse him or herself. The ruins were covered with morning glories when I saw them, and it was wonderful to think that Mary had used one of these *mikvot.*

The law required that the woman who came to be purified after childbirth should offer a lamb and a turtledove. However, if the family was poor, she could offer two turtledoves instead. Luke is reminding us that Jesus was born into a poor family.

> When the time came for their purification according to the law of Moses, they brought him up to Jerusalem to present him to the Lord (as it is written in the law of the Lord, "Every firstborn male shall be designated as holy to the Lord"), and they offered a sacrifice according to what is stated in the law of the Lord, "a pair of turtledoves or two young pigeons."
>
> *Luke 2:22-24*

Luke, the Gentile, likes to present the Jewish people in the best possible light, so he shows the Holy Family being met in the temple by an old man, Simeon. Simeon represents all the people of the Old Testament who were eagerly awaiting the new thing God would do in sending the Messiah. He was of an age where death seemed close, but God had told him that he would witness something wonderful before he died. He was living his final days focused on the future, not on the past. Let's meet Simeon.

> Now there was a man in Jerusalem whose name was Simeon; this man was righteous and devout, looking for-

ward to the consolation of Israel, and the Holy Spirit rested on him. It had been revealed to him by the Holy Spirit that he would not see death before he had seen the Lord's Messiah.

Luke 2:25-26

—⁓—

Simeon was a man so holy, so attuned to God's presence in his life, that he was led by the Spirit into the Temple at precisely the moment when the Holy Family came bringing the Child. He recognized Jesus, and took him into his arms. This was the greatest joy of his life.

At last he is ready for death, willing to let go of this life. He prays the *Nunc Dimittis,* the prayer the church uses in the Divine Office as a preparation for sleep every night. We can hope to be able to pray it when the time comes for our death.

The wisdom of this prayer is that of a holy man at the final stage of his growth. It is a personal prayer, but also one of extraordinary insight into the wider world. In the Jewish temple, this old Jew, lover of Jewish ways, proclaims that this Jewish baby is to be "a light to the Gentiles." In fact, he summarizes the whole of Luke's two volumes, the Gospel and Acts. Jesus has come to be both the glory of Israel and a light to the pagan nations, to bring to an end the hostility that has always existed between the two. Paul will say, in Acts, that as an apostle he is called to be a light to the nations, fulfilling Simeon's prophecy (Acts 13:47).

Guided by the Spirit, Simeon came into the temple; and when the parents brought in the child Jesus, to do for him what was customary under the law, Simeon took him into his arms and praised God, saying:
"Master, now you are dismissing your servant in
    peace,
        according to your word,
    for my eyes have seen your salvation,

which you have prepared in the presence of all
peoples,
a light for revelation to the Gentiles,
and for glory to your people Israel."

Luke 2:27-32

—···—

Mary and Joseph were amazed at what Simeon said about
their child. Mary still had much to learn about her son.

Simeon blessed Joseph and Mary, but addressed a further prophecy to Mary alone. After Joseph's death, it is she
who will share in the suffering of her adult son. Here we
have the first dark note in Luke's joyous Gospel. The
shadow of the cross rests on this infant.

> And the child's father and mother were amazed at what
> was being said about him. Then Simeon blessed them and
> said to his mother Mary, "This child is destined for the
> falling and the rising of many in Israel, and to be a sign that
> will be opposed so that the inner thoughts of many will be
> revealed—and a sword will pierce your own soul too."

Luke 2:33-35

—···—

Often in his Gospel Luke will tell parallel stories about a man
and a woman. In a world where women received little
respect, this was shocking. Now he brings an old woman into
the temple to represent the Jewish people in welcoming the
new Child, just as Simeon had done. They also represent all
old people who are wise and unselfish enough to give way to
the new, to welcome it with joy.

Luke emphasizes that Anna was a widow because Jesus
had shown a special interest in widows, and because widows were an important group in the church he knew.
Widows did not ordinarily inherit their husband's property,
so they were among the poor for whom God had special
care. The early church provided for the widows, and grad-

ually formed them into a group that had a special role of prayer and service in the community. It has been suggested that one of these widows provided Luke with some of the many stories about widows in his Gospel. Whether that is true or not, it is clear that Luke likes to include stories that will be an encouragement to the widows in the church of his time.

The widow Anna not only recognizes the infant as the Messiah, but also goes out immediately to "get on the telephone" to spread the good news through her network of devout Jews. She is the very first evangelist, and reminds us of the women who would be the first to spread the good news of the resurrection.

> There was also a prophet, Anna the daughter of Phanuel, of the tribe of Asher. She was of a great age, having lived with her husband seven years after her marriage, then as a widow to the age of eighty-four. She never left the temple but worshiped there with fasting and prayer night and day. At that moment she came, and began to praise God and to speak about the child to all who were looking for the redemption of Jerusalem.
>
> *Luke 2:36-38*

Luke ends his story by emphasizing yet again that the parents of Jesus carefully fulfilled the obligations of the Law. This was a good reminder to the Gentile Christians for whom he wrote that they should have respect for the Jewish Christians who still observed the Law, even though they as Gentiles were not required to do so.

Then he tells us that Jesus, like John the Baptist, and like every other child, grew. This was more than physical growth. He also grew in wisdom; he learned things. It is a reminder to us that Jesus, though he is God, is also truly a human being. And to be human is not to know it all, but to learn throughout one's life.

When they had finished everything required by the law of the Lord, they returned to Galilee, to their own town of Nazareth. The child grew and became strong, filled with wisdom; and the favor of God was upon him.

Luke 2:39-40

Questions for Reflection

1. How do you think we should celebrate the birth of Jesus at Christmas?

2. Who in our society is looked down on, as shepherds were in Mary's time?

3. Do Simeon or Anna remind you of someone you know? Why?

3. When in your life have you felt the Spirit guided you, like Simeon, to be in a particular place at a particular time for an important reason?

4. Simeon did not feel ready for death until he held the Christ Child in his arms. Is there something that needs to happen before you feel ready for death?

5. Widows had a special role in the early church. In what ways is that true of widows in the church today? In what ways should it be true?

6. Anna spread the news about Jesus. How do you and people you know spread the word about Jesus today?

7. Luke emphasizes that Jesus grew in wisdom and age and favor before God and people. In what ways do you feel that you are still growing?

Suggestions for Further Reading

Matthew 1, 2: A different version of the infancy of Jesus, from Joseph's point of view.

Luke 24:1-11: About proclaiming the resurrection

Luke 7:11-17; Luke 18:1-8; Luke 21:1-4; Acts 6:1-6; Acts 9: About widows

CHAPTER THREE

Preparation for Ministry

A Second Journey to Jerusalem

THE BIBLICAL LAW REQUIRED THAT EVERY Jewish man make the pilgrimage to the Jerusalem temple three times a year. Mary was accustomed to going with her husband at these holy times. Pilgrims would travel in groups, singing psalms and sharing their enthusiasm about their faith as pilgrims do. At twelve, an age that was bordering on adulthood in those days, Jesus was allowed to come with them.

> Now every year his parents went to Jerusalem for the festival of the Passover. And when he was twelve years old, they went up as usual for the festival.
>
> *Luke 2:41-42*

This last story about the young Jesus is one to touch the hearts of all parents of teenagers. It is a story of a runaway teenager, with a twist.

Jesus is that troublesome being, an adolescent. He is not a child, nor is he really an adult. He comes with his parents from the little town of Nazareth to celebrate Passover in Jerusalem, and becomes so enthralled with the life of the big city that he does not join the Nazareth caravan for their return. Men and women traveled separately in the caravan, coming together only at the end of the day. Joseph presumes Jesus, like other children, is with his mother. Mary, sensitive to her son's growing up, presumes he is with his father and the other men. Any parent can imagine their terror when they discover he has been left behind.

And any parent can understand Mary's indignant words

when they finally find him. Only a teenager could understand his response. He is completely engrossed in the new world he is discovering, and really cannot imagine why they are concerned about him.

In this story we see that Mary is amazed at seeing Jesus with the doctors in the temple, just as she was amazed at Simeon's prophecy. Luke paints her as the model Christian. We should all be frequently amazed at the new things God keeps doing.

In this last story of the Infancy Narrative, Luke is preparing us for the final chapters of his Gospel. As Jesus at this Passover time is lost for three days and then found, at his final Passover he will be in the tomb three days and then rise.

> When the festival was ended and they started to return, the boy Jesus stayed behind in Jerusalem, but his parents did not know it. Assuming that he was in the group of travelers, they went a day's journey. Then they started to look for him among their relatives and friends. When they did not find him, they returned to Jerusalem to search for him. After three days they found him in the temple, sitting among the teachers, listening to them and asking them questions. And all who heard him were amazed at his understanding and his answers. When his parents saw him they were astonished; and his mother said to him, "Child why have you treated us like this? Look, your father and I have been searching for you in great anxiety." He said to them, "Why were you searching for me? Did you not know that I must be in my Father's house?" But they did not understand what he said to them.

Luke 2:43-50

The story of the finding of the Child Jesus in the Temple gives us a vivid glimpse into Jesus' identity. Mary says, "Your father and I have been searching for you." But Jesus is aware of another father: "I must be in my Father's house."

Mary ponders all these things in her heart. She is our model. We can never finish pondering the life of Jesus, and God's actions in our own lives.

After his adolescent adventure, Jesus returns and becomes again the obedient son. Again we are told that he grew.

> Then he went down with them and came to Nazareth, and was obedient to them. His mother treasured all these things in her heart.
> And Jesus increased in wisdom and in years, and in divine and human favor.
>
> *Luke 2:51-52*

John Begins His Ministry

In the next chapter we will hear about the beginning of Jesus' adult ministry. But first, of course, we have to hear about the beginning of the ministry of John the Baptist. The son of Elizabeth and Zechariah has grown up, and the promise made about him by the angel Gabriel is about to be fulfilled. Luke wants to set the event in time, but he has no B.C. and A.D. dates! He dates it, as was customary, in relation to the rulers of the time, both secular and religious. These are names we will meet again in the account of Jesus' Passion: Herod, Pilate, Annas, and Caiaphas. Annas actually held the office of high priest only from A.D. 6 till A.D. 15, but after his retirement he was followed in the office by five sons and a son-in-law, Caiaphas. He seems to have continued on as a sort of power behind the throne or high priest emeritus, still exerting great influence. In our terms, the date Luke is setting is probably A.D. 28 or 29.

> In the fifteenth year of the reign of Emperor Tiberius, when Pontius Pilate was governor of Judea, and Herod

was ruler of Galilee, and his brother Philip ruler of the region of Ituraea and Trachonitis, and Lysanias ruler of Abilene, during the high priesthood of Annas and Caiaphas, the word of God came to John son of Zechariah in the wilderness.

Luke 3:1-2

John's role was to be a prophetic voice crying out in the wilderness. The wilderness, or desert, was the place in which Israel was spiritually formed for forty years when Moses led them out of Egypt. By John's time, most Israelites lived in cities or on farms, but he was calling them, symbolically, to return to that time in the wilderness when God had been close to them. This was more than a geographic change; he was calling them to conversion. Sometimes we, too, have to leave our ordinary setting and go to some place of retreat where we can hear the Lord's challenge.

As a symbol of a changed life, John called the people to baptism. They knew nothing about a sacrament called "baptism." To them, the word simply meant "immersion." Each person who responded to John's preaching was thoroughly immersed in the Jordan River. The place where John was preaching was not far from the monastery of Qumran, where fervent Jews formed a community, to which John the Baptist may have belonged at one time. Those joining the Qumran community were initiated by a ritual immersion. However, this immersion, like other Jewish ritual purifications, was something a person did himself. The baptism of John, like the later Christian baptism, was administered by someone else. It was a surrender to the action of God, not a thing one could do on one's own.

He went into all the region around the Jordan, proclaiming a baptism of repentance for the forgiveness of sins, as it is written in the book of the words of the prophet Isaiah,

"The voice of one crying out in the wilderness:
'Prepare the way of the Lord,
    make his paths straight.
Every valley shall be filled,
    and every mountain and hill shall be made low,
and the crooked shall be made straight,
    and the rough ways made smooth:
and all flesh shall see the salvation of God.'"

Luke 3:4-6

———

John was as fiery as any Old Testament prophet. Isaiah had told the Jews that they were like stones hewn from the great rock, Abraham (Isaiah 51:1,2). They were proud of that, and looked down on those who were not privileged to be descended from Abraham. But John tells them that God can raise up children of Abraham from the very rocks in the bed of the River Jordan. Luke's Gentile readers knew they were these unexpected children of Abraham. God can make children of Abraham from the most unlikely material. The further implication is that any of us Christians who are proud to be children of Abraham, can, like the Jews, be cut off if we do not bear fruit by changing our lives according to God's call. We are not God's only resource.

> John said to the crowds that came out to be baptized by him, "You brood of vipers! Who warned you to flee from the wrath to come? Bear fruits worthy of repentance. Do not begin to say to yourselves, 'We have Abraham as our ancestor'; for I tell you, God is able from these stones to raise up children to Abraham. Even now the ax is lying at the root of the trees; every tree therefore that does not bear good fruit is cut down and thrown into the fire."

Luke 3:7-9

———

Next we have some specific information about the advice given by John, which only Luke records. The people listening were shaken, and asked what it was they must do. (Any preacher can tell you that the test of a good sermon is not whether people come afterward and praise you for your eloquence, but whether they ask you, or themselves, "What should I do?") John's reply is surprisingly down-to-earth, like the message of the Old Testament prophets. You must share what you have with those in need. This is a favorite theme of Luke's, part of his concern for the poor.

Amazingly, even tax collectors, who were so hated by the Jews that they were not allowed in the synagogues, came to hear John, and asked what they were to do. John did not demand that they abandon the work that made them such outcasts. He simply told them to perform it honestly. Soldiers came, too, and were not told to leave the army, but to refrain from misusing their power and from taking bribes. John anticipated the message of Jesus by showing that God invites even the hated tax collectors and soldiers into the kingdom.

> And the crowds asked him, "What then should we do?" In reply he said to them, "Whoever has two coats must share with anyone who has none; and whoever has food must do likewise." Even tax collectors came to be baptized, and they asked him, "Teacher, what should we do?" He said to them, "Collect no more than the amount prescribed for you." Soldiers also asked him, "And we, what should we do?" He said to them, "Do not extort money from anyone by threats or false accusation, and be satisfied with your wages."

Luke 3:10-14

In the Infancy Narrative, Luke was concerned to clarify the role of John as someone who was important not in himself, but because he was to prepare the way for Jesus. Here we see John himself saying the same thing. He did not fall into the temptation of popular public figures who let the adulation of their public give them a false sense of their own importance. John knew clearly what he was and what he was not, a grace we might all pray for. The church has a lovely way of clarifying his particular mission by assigning June 24, just after the summer solstice, as his birth date. His words "that I may decrease and he may increase" (John 3:30) are echoed by the sun, which grows weaker after June 24 and stronger after the winter solstice, so close to Jesus' assigned birthday of December 25.

His understanding of Jesus was less clear. He does not seem to have known that the Messiah would come twice, once in a humble form, and later as all-powerful judge. John is focused on the Second Coming, when Jesus will separate the good from the bad as a farmer in Israel separated the wheat from the chaff with a winnowing fork.

> As the people were filled with expectation, and all were questioning in their hearts concerning John, whether he might be the Messiah, John answered all of them by saying, "I baptize you with water; but one who is more powerful than I is coming; I am not worthy to untie the thong of his sandals. He will baptize you with the Holy Spirit and fire. His winnowing fork is in his hand, to clear his threshing floor and to gather the wheat into his granary; but the chaff he will burn with unquenchable fire."
>
> So, with many other exhortations, he proclaimed the good news to the people.

Luke 3:15-18

The people, even the tax collectors and soldiers, welcome the message of John. For them, the call to repentance is good news. But those in authority are not so open. In this John has the same experience Jesus will have. John prepares the way for Jesus in his birth, his preaching, his rejection, his imprisonment, and, eventually, his death.

But Herod the ruler, who had been rebuked by him because of Herodias, his brother's wife, and because of all the evil things that Herod had done, added to them all by shutting up John in prison.

Luke 3:19-20

The Baptism of Jesus

At this point, John leaves the stage, and Luke shifts his focus to Jesus. We are privileged here to witness a scene of Jesus at prayer. Jesus' baptism by John is mentioned, but Luke does not focus on it. For him, it is primarily the background of the prayer experience in which Jesus is empowered for his mission. Later, Luke will show the early Christians gathered in prayer at Pentecost, when they are empowered for their mission. He wants his readers to turn to prayer before they begin any ministry.

Now when all the people were baptized, and when Jesus also had been baptized and was praying, the heaven was opened, and the Holy Spirit descended upon him in bodily form like a dove. And a voice came from heaven, "You are my Son, the Beloved; with you I am well pleased."

Luke 3:21-22

The Temptations of Jesus

We might expect that Jesus would go directly from this great prayer experience into his ministry. Instead, the Spirit he had just received led him deep into that same place where the people of Israel and John the Baptist had been formed: the wilderness. As Israel had been tested in the wilderness for forty years, Jesus would be tested for forty days.

The wilderness of Judea is a desolate place, and it is hard for one traveling through it today to imagine how anyone could have lived there alone for forty days without food or water. Jesus did. Being human, he was weakened by the ordeal. It was when he was most weak that the devil attacked him. The devil is clever. A truly holy person is not likely to be tempted by wicked things. Such a person will want only to respond to the call of God. The devil's only hope was to induce Jesus to respond to that call in a way that is not God's way. Jesus knew that he had received power from God to fulfill his mission. The three temptations only suggest that he use that power in a way that God does not intend. First, that he use it to fill his own human needs so he will be able to go about his work.

> Jesus, full of the Holy Spirit, returned from the Jordan and was led by the Spirit in the wilderness, where for forty days he was tempted by the devil. He ate nothing at all during those days, and when they were over, he was famished. The devil said to him, "If you are the Son of God, command this stone to become a loaf of bread." Jesus answered him, "It is written, 'One does not live by bread alone.' "

> *Luke 4:1-4*

Second, the devil suggests a shortcut. Jesus is called to rule over all nations. But how is this to be accomplished? The devil suggests a quick and effective way, far from the centuries of painful struggle that it would actually take. It is the way of idolatry, that is, giving first place to someone or something other than God.

> Then the devil led him up and showed him in an instant all the kingdoms of the world. And the devil said to him, "To you I will give their glory and all this authority; for it has been given over to me, and I give it to anyone I please. If you, then, will worship me, it will all be yours." Jesus

answered him, "It is written,
   'Worship the Lord your God,
     and serve only him.'"

Luke 4:5-8

As a climax, the devil takes Jesus to the Jerusalem temple, which has such special importance throughout Luke's Gospel. Now he is tempted to gain the support he needs from the people by a spectacular miracle. He even quotes Scripture to support his argument. (Perhaps we should be warned that not everyone who quotes Scripture is to be trusted.) But Jesus knows that this is not God's way. Perhaps this is the greatest temptation. Jesus was tempted first to use his power over material objects, next over people, lastly over God. What on the surface looked like a great act of trust in God was actually an attempt to manipulate God.

> Then the devil took him to Jerusalem, and placed him on the pinnacle of the temple, saying to him, "If you are the Son of God, throw yourself down from here, for it is written,
>   'He will command his angels concerning you,
>   to protect you,'
> and
>   'On their hands they will bear you up,
>   so that you will not dash your foot against a
>   stone.'"
> Jesus answered him, "It is said, 'Do not put the Lord your God to the test.'" When the devil had finished every test, he departed from him until an opportune time.

Luke 4:9-13

Jesus Begins His Ministry

After thirty or so years of humble life in Nazareth, participation in John's baptism, and the ordeal of testing in the desert, Jesus is finally ready to begin the work to which he is called. At a time when few people lived beyond forty, he was of mature years. All this can be a comfort to us when we feel God's work in our lives is moving slowly.

> Then Jesus, filled with the power of the Spirit, returned to Galilee, and a report about him spread through all the surrounding country. He began to teach in their synagogues and was praised by everyone.

Luke 4:14-15

Questions for Reflection

1. When have you, or someone you know, been as amazed at the behavior of an adolescent child as Mary and Joseph were at Jesus talking with the teachers in the temple?

2. Mary pondered in her heart the things concerning her son, knowing she did not fully understand them. What are you still pondering, knowing you do not fully understand?

3. How do you think you would have responded to a preacher like John the Baptist?

4. Why do you think Jesus, who was without sin, chose to undergo a baptism of repentance?

5. What temptations can you think of in modern life that are like any of the temptations of Christ?

Suggestions for Further Reading

Mark 6:17-29: Fuller account of the martyrdom of John the Baptist

Numbers, Chapters 11, 12, 13, 14; Psalm 95: The temptation of Israel in the wilderness

CHAPTER FOUR

The Ministry Begins

Jesus in Nazareth

AFTER HIS PREPARATION IN THE DESERT, Jesus preached in synagogues throughout Galilee. His message was welcomed everywhere. Finally, he arrived back at his hometown. He came to the Sabbath service, as he always did. He was asked to serve as lector, and agreed. However, he did not just read the passage that was pointed out to him, but searched through the scroll until he found the passage he wanted. As was customary, he read standing, but sat down afterward to explain the passage.

This is the first sermon of Jesus that Luke records, and it is a kind of inauguration speech or mission statement. Looking back, it connects Jesus with the prophecy of Isaiah. Looking forward, it points to all that will happen in Jesus' public life.

> When he came to Nazareth, where he had been brought up, he went to the synagogue on the Sabbath day, as was his custom. He stood up to read, and the scroll of the prophet Isaiah was given to him. He unrolled the scroll and found the place where it was written:
>
> "The Spirit of the Lord is upon me,
>   because he has anointed me
>   to bring good news to the poor.
> He has sent me to proclaim release to the captives
>   and recovery of sight to the blind,
>   to let the oppressed go free,
> to proclaim the year of the Lord's favor."
>
> And he rolled up the scroll, gave it back to the attendant, and sat down. The eyes of all in the synagogue were fixed on him. Then he began to say to them, "Today

45

this Scripture has been fulfilled in your hearing."

Luke 4:16-21

The people of Nazareth, who have known Jesus from his infancy, react to his new role in a strange way. At first they are amazed at how well this son of the local carpenter has spoken. But their acceptance is not wholehearted and does not last long.

Jesus laments at the rejection he feels from those he has known so well and so long. This is the beginning of the rejection he will experience from his own people throughout his life, culminating in his death.

He wants to show them that, though he is teaching new and shocking things, his teaching is rooted in the Scripture they all know. Therefore, he tells two stories from the Scripture. It is typical of Luke that one of the stories is about a woman and one about a man. In both stories, a prophet reaches out to a Gentile, someone who is not part of the Jewish faith community. Already Jesus is pointing toward the story Luke will tell in the Acts of the Apostles, where Jesus is preached to the Gentiles, causing much offense among his Jewish followers. Simeon had prophesied that Jesus would be a light to the Gentiles (Luke 2:32), but this is the first time this idea has been hinted at in a synagogue. The idea of outreach to Gentiles enrages the narrow-minded people of Nazareth, and they turn totally against Jesus, even trying to kill him. They represent people of all ages who are unwilling to share God's gift to them with people different from themselves.

All spoke well of him and were amazed at the gracious words that came from his mouth. They said, "Is not this Joseph's son?" He said to them, "Doubtless you will quote to me this proverb, 'Doctor, cure yourself!' And you will say, 'Do here also in your hometown the things that we have heard you did at Capernaum.' " And he said, "Truly I tell you, no prophet is accepted in the prophet's hometown. But the truth is, there were many widows in Israel in the time of Elijah, when the heaven was shut up three years and six months, and there was a severe famine over all the land; yet Elijah was sent to none of them except to a widow at Zarephath in Sidon. There were also many lepers in Israel in the time of the prophet Elisha, and none of them was cleansed except Naaman the Syrian." When they heard this, all in the synagogue were filled with rage. They got up, drove him out of the town, and led him to the brow of the hill on which their town was built, so that they might hurl him off the cliff. But he passed through the midst of them and went on his way.

Luke 4:22-30

Jesus in Capernaum

Jesus then went to Capernaum and preached in the synagogue there. There Simon (who would later be called Peter) heard him, and invited him home after the service. Presumably, Simon's wife was preparing the Sabbath meal, to which guests were often invited. But her mother was unable to help because she was suffering from a fever. Since she was living in her son-in-law's home, she was probably an elderly widow with no sons of her own, an object of pity in the town. Jesus spoke firmly to the fever, and it left her. Immediately, she got up and began to help with serving the meal. Luke speaks elsewhere (Luke 8:2) of other women healed by Jesus who showed their gratitude for the health he restored to them by providing for his needs and those of his disciples. Luke points them out as models all Christians should follow.

After leaving the synagogue he entered Simon's house. Now Simon's mother-in-law was suffering from a high fever, and they asked him about her. Then he stood over her and rebuked the fever, and it left her. Immediately she got up and began to serve them.

Luke 4:38–39

The Call of Peter

Peter probably did a good bit of thinking about the cure of his mother-in-law. He was being prepared for his call. It was to come in three stages. First, Jesus asks him a simple favor. The crowds who wanted to listen to Jesus were crowding around him so closely that it was hard for anybody to hear his words. Jesus asks Peter to let him use his fishing boat as a podium. Willingly, Peter rows out a short distance from the shore. The water carries Jesus' voice, so everyone can hear. Peter, crouched in his boat, listens intently.

The second stage of Peter's call comes when Jesus has finished speaking and decides to return Peter's favor by giving him the great catch of fish of which every fisher dreams. All Peter has to do is let the nets out. But Peter knows his trade. Fish, even today, can be caught in the Sea of Galilee (which Luke calls the lake of Gennesaret) at night, not in the daylight. Anyway, Peter is weary and frustrated because he has worked hard all the previous night, and caught not a thing. He has no energy for a fool's task like putting the nets down in broad daylight. Within him, the competence born of long experience struggles with a newly budding faith in Jesus. The faith wins out, and he pulls up an extraordinary catch. It is a turning point in Peter's life. He is overwhelmed with an awe and love for Jesus that will never leave him. But deep contact with God has a side effect of making one aware of one's own sinfulness, as can be seen in the lives of many saints. The shock makes Peter say, "Go away from me, Lord, for I am a sinful man."

Jesus knows better than to take Peter at his word. Instead, he proceeds to the third stage of the call. He tells

Peter not to be afraid, because what he has seen is only a preview of his life's real work, which will be catching people, not mere fish. Peter knows then that Jesus is calling him to something beyond his wildest dreams, and he leaves everything and follows him. Peter was not a young man making a decision about the direction of his life. He had a home and family and business, a lot to leave behind. The story reminds us readers that the call of Jesus to leave everything behind and make a radically new start can come at any time of life.

Once while Jesus was standing beside the lake of Gennesaret, and the crowd was pressing in on him to hear the word of God, he saw two boats there at the shore of the lake; the fishermen had gone out of them and were washing their nets. He got into one of the boats, the one belonging to Simon, and asked him to put out a little way from the shore. Then he sat down and taught the crowds from the boat. When he had finished speaking, he said to Simon, "Put out into the deep water and let down your nets for a catch." Simon answered, "Master, we have worked all night long but have caught nothing. Yet if you say so, I will let down the nets." When they had done this, they caught so many fish that their nets were beginning to break. So they signaled their partners in the other boat to come and help them. And they came and filled both boats, so that they began to sink. But when Simon Peter saw it, he fell down at Jesus' knees, saying, "Go away from me, Lord, for I am a sinful man!" For he and all who were with him were amazed at the catch of fish that they had taken; and so also were James and John, sons of Zebedee, who were partners with Simon. Then Jesus said to Simon, "Do not be afraid; from now on you will be catching people." When they had brought their boats to shore, they left everything and followed him.

Luke 5:1-11

———

The Call of the Twelve

Luke always stresses Jesus' prayer, because he wants his readers to be motivated to lead prayerful lives, and especially to pray before making major decisions. Jesus spent a whole night in prayer before selecting the twelve apostles. Jesus had crowds of disciples, that is, people who followed him and learned from him. From them he chose only twelve apostles, that is, authorized representatives he would send out to establish the church.

Of these twelve, he gave a new name to only one. Simon became Peter. This was not a proper name that had ever belonged to anyone; it was simply the word "rock." One paraphrase of the Gospel calls him "Rocky." Matthew (Matthew 16:18) will explain that Peter was the rock on which Jesus would build his church.

The names of the twelve apostles are different in different lists, but each list begins with Peter and ends with Judas, the traitor. The church never forgot Judas because he reminds us that even those specially called by God are vulnerable to temptation.

> Now during those days he went out to the mountain to pray; and he spent the night in prayer to God. And when day came, he called his disciples and chose twelve of them, whom he also named apostles: Simon, whom he named Peter, and his brother Andrew, and James, and John, and Philip, and Bartholomew, and Matthew, and Thomas, and James son of Alphaeus, and Simon, who was called the Zealot, and Judas son of James, and Judas Iscariot, who became a traitor.
>
> He came down with them and stood on a level place, with a great crowd of his disciples and a great multitude of people from all Judea, Jerusalem, and the coast of Tyre and Sidon. They had come to hear him and to be healed of their diseases; and those who were troubled with unclean spirits were cured. And all in the crowd were trying to touch him, for power came out from him and healed all of them.

Luke 6:12-19

—⁓—

The Beatitudes

A part of the sermon that Jesus then gave is the Beatitudes. Matthew's version of the Beatitudes is better known than Luke's. Only in Luke are there four beatitudes and four woes contrasted to them. This theme of how God reverses human values is dear to Luke. He introduced it in Mary's song of praise (Luke 1:51-53). It seems that Jesus has learned something from his mother! Luke's version of the Beatitudes shows Jesus overturning not only the secular values of his time, but also some of the religious values. Jews of his time, like some Christians today, believed that wealth was a sign of God's favor (see, for example, Deuteronomy 28). Jesus says just the opposite.

> Then he looked up at his disciples and said:
> "Blessed are you who are poor,
>   for yours is the kingdom of God.
> "Blessed are you who are hungry now,
>   for you will be filled.
> "Blessed are you who weep now,
>   for you will laugh.
> "Blessed are you when people hate you, and when they exclude you, revile you, and defame you on account of the Son of Man. Rejoice in that day and leap for joy, for surely your reward is great in heaven; for that is what their ancestors did to the prophets.
> "But woe to you who are rich,
>   for you have received your consolation.
> "Woe to you who are full now,
>   for you will be hungry.
> "Woe to you who are laughing now,
>   for you will mourn and weep.
> "Woe to you when all speak well of you, for that is what their ancestors did to the false prophets.

Luke 6:20-26

—///—

The Centurion

A centurion was an officer in the Roman army, a representative of the oppressive power of Rome. But the two centurions mentioned in the Gospel, one in this story and one at the crucifixion, are both admirable characters. They prepare us for the centurions who will play very positive roles in the Acts of the Apostles (10:1-49; 22:25-26; 27:1-44). This centurion was that rare being: a colonial administrator actually loved by the people he governs.

> After Jesus had finished all his sayings in the hearing of the people, he entered Capernaum. A centurion there had a slave whom he valued highly, and who was ill and close to death. When he heard about Jesus, he sent some Jewish elders to him, asking him to come and heal his slave. When they came to Jesus, they appealed to him earnestly, saying, "He is worthy of having you do this for him, for he loves our people, and it is he who built our synagogue for us."

> *Luke 7:1-5*

The centurion knew the ways of power. He did not have to be physically present in a place to make something happen there. He believed Jesus had greater power than his. So he did not ask Jesus to come into his home, where he might have incurred ritual defilement. He believed Jesus could heal his slave from a distance, and Jesus did so.

> And Jesus went with them, but when he was not far from the house, the centurion sent friends to say to him, "Lord, do not trouble yourself, for I am not worthy to have you come under my roof; therefore I did not presume to come to you. But only speak the word, and let my servant be healed. For I also am a man set under authority, with soldiers under me; and I say to one, 'Go.' and he goes, and to another, 'Come,' and he comes, and to my slave, 'Do this,'

and the slave does it." When Jesus heard this he was amazed at him, and turning to the crowd that followed him, he said, "I tell you, not even in Israel have I found such faith." When those who had been sent returned to the house, they found the slave in good health.

Luke 7:6-10

Raising of the Widow's Son

Jesus seems to seek out the poorest, those most marginalized in the society. Women were always second-class citizens in Jesus' world, but they had some place in society through their fathers, husbands, or sons. An elderly widow who had no son was the most pitiful person imaginable. This is the story of such a woman. Jesus raised her son to life for her sake, to restore her to her place in the community. Perhaps he was thinking of his own mother, another widow who was soon to lose her only son. We do not know how the son felt about his recall. Only Luke tells the story of this widow.

Soon afterwards he went to a town called Nain, and his disciples and a large crowd went with him. As he approached the gate of the town, a man who had died was being carried out. He was his mother's only son, and she was a widow; and with her was a large crowd from the town. When the Lord saw her, he had compassion for her and said to her, "Do not weep." Then he came forward and touched the bier, and the bearers stood still. And he said, "Young man, I say to you, rise!" The dead man sat up and began to speak, and Jesus gave him to his mother. Fear seized all of them; and they glorified God, saying, "A great prophet has risen among us!" and "God has looked favorably on his people!" This word about him spread throughout Judea and all the surrounding country.

Luke 7:11-17

Questions For Reflection

1. How do you think Mary felt about Jesus' visit to the Nazareth synagogue?

2. Jesus went up a mountain to pray all night before selecting his twelve apostles. How do you prepare to make a major decision?

3. What kind of person do you think Peter was? What in Scripture makes you think that?

4. Peter was called to be a fisher of people. What do you think you are called to be?

5. What people can you think of who exemplify either the Beatitudes or the Woes?

Suggestions for Further Reading

1 Kings 17:8-24; 2 Kings 5:1-19: The stories to which Jesus refers at Nazareth

Matthew 5:1-12: Matthew's version of the Beatitudes

Matthew 16:13-26: The meaning of Peter's name

CHAPTER FIVE

John the Baptist Again, and a Sinful Woman

JOHN HAD ENDED HIS PUBLIC MINISTRY at the time Jesus began his. Herod had put him in prison. We do not hear anything about John's growth and struggles in this time of enforced retirement except one poignant passage. Clearly, in his prison John has heard about Jesus' activities. This austere man of the desert, fiery preacher, cannot have felt completely comfortable with Jesus' gentle ways, healing the sick, restoring to a widow her dead son, joining the ordinary folk in their synagogues and their homes, eating and drinking with them. Any of us who have put all our passion into serving God in a particular way can find it hard to respect those who serve in quite a different way.

John knew that his role was to prepare for someone much greater than himself. He had envisioned that one as a fiery judge somewhat like himself who would come with a winnowing fork to clear the threshing floor and burn the chaff with unquenchable fire (Luke 3:16, 17). Could this gentle preacher be the one? He was perplexed. Though his public appearance had been one of a forceful person sure of his message, in prison he shows himself humble, willing to learn even things that do not fit comfortably with what he has known so far. It can happen to holy people like John that toward the end of their lives they are attacked by doubt, and need the support of others. Instead of pretending to the disciples who still come to him that he knows the answers, he sends them to Jesus with a question.

Jesus is sensitive to his cousin's spiritual crisis. He knows how feeble his own ministry appears compared to John's. He cannot adopt John's style, or pretend to. He can

only send the messengers back with a quotation from
Isaiah that shows that there is room in God's plan for his
kind of ministry as well as for John's kind. He was inviting
John to do what we so often have to do: look at the parts
of Scripture that do not fit into our preconceived ideas. We
are not told how John responded, whether he could rise to
the challenge of a Messiah so different from the one he had
expected.

> The disciples of John reported all these things to him.
> So John summoned two of his disciples and sent them to
> the Lord to ask, "Are you the one who is to come, or are we
> to wait for another?" When the men had come to him, they
> said, "John the Baptist has sent us to you to ask, 'Are you the
> one who is to come, or are we to wait for another?'" Jesus
> had just then cured many people of diseases, plagues, and
> evil spirits, and had given sight to many who were blind.
> And he answered them, "Go and tell John what you have
> seen and heard: the blind receive their sight, the lame
> walk, the lepers are cleansed, the deaf hear, the dead are
> raised, the poor have good news brought to them. And
> blessed is anyone who takes no offense at me."

Luke 7:18-23

We have just seen the uncertainty of John's attitude toward
Jesus. Now Jesus tells us clearly what he thinks of John. A
lesser person might have been offended by John's rough
ways, his lack of tact, his hesitation to accept Jesus. Jesus has
only words of praise for this prophet so different from himself, yet sent to prepare the way for him. He risks the anger of
Herod Antipas who has imprisoned John by his wholehearted support of the prisoner.

> When John's messengers had gone, Jesus began to
> speak to the crowds about John: "What did you go out into
> the wilderness to look at? A reed shaken by the wind?

What then did you go out to see? Someone dressed in soft robes? Look, those who put on fine clothing and live in luxury are in royal palaces. What then did you go out to see? A prophet? Yes, I tell you, and more than a prophet. This is the one about whom it is written,
'See, I am sending my messenger ahead of you,
who will prepare your way before you.'

I tell you, among those born of women no one is greater than John; yet the least in the kingdom of God is greater than he."

Luke 7:24-28

The common people listening to Jesus, including even marginalized groups like the tax collectors, had accepted the harsh message of John, and accepted also the gentle message of Jesus. The professionally religious, on the other hand, could accept neither John nor Jesus. Each step on the spiritual journey prepares us for the next, even though we may not have been able to imagine the second step when we took the first. Those who had refused the challenge of John were not ready for the challenge of Jesus.

Jesus goes on to illustrate with a vivid story that those unwilling to hear God's message will not hear it whether it comes in the fiery words of John or the gentle ones of Jesus. Jesus knew about children's games. They played at the things their parents did seriously: weddings and funerals. The children in this little story invited other children to play "wedding." When they did not respond, they invited them to play "funeral." They did not respond to that either, as the Pharisees did not respond either to the message of John or to that of Jesus.

Sometimes those fervent for finding new ways to spread the Gospel need to remember this story.

(And all the people who heard this, including the tax

collectors, acknowledged the justice of God, because they had been baptized with John's baptism. But by refusing to be baptized by him, the Pharisees and the lawyers rejected God's purpose for themselves.)

"To what then will I compare the people of this generation, and what are they like? They are like children sitting in the marketplace and calling to one another,

'We played the flute for you, and you did not dance;
we wailed, and you did not weep.'

For John the Baptist has come eating no bread and drinking no wine, and you say, 'He has a demon'; the Son of Man has come eating and drinking, and you say, 'Look, a glutton and a drunkard, a friend of tax collectors and sinners!'

Luke 7:29-34

The next story shows Jesus befriending a sinful woman in a way that might have shocked John the Baptist. A Pharisee named Simon invited Jesus to a meal at his home. The invitation showed that he had some openness to Jesus. At least he was curious about this popular preacher, and wanted to hear for himself what he was saying. We never learn what his final decision was. The story is not really about him.

Jesus enters the dining room, where couches were arranged around a U-shaped table. Each guest reclined with head by the table, and feet stretched out behind. No one sat inside the U; servers came and went there.

A woman with a bad reputation in the town enters the dining room. This woman is not named, and there is no reason to identify her with Mary Magdalene or Mary of Bethany. She may well have been a prostitute, though Luke does not say so specifically. Luke always stresses Jesus' concern for the poor, and no one was poorer than women forced into prostitution because they had no man to support them. They might become economically well off, enough to own an expensive alabaster flask of ointment. But this could never make up for the contempt in which the highly moral Jewish society held them.

We can feel the Pharisee Simon stiffen as this woman enters his home, presumably bringing ritual impurity with her. But she pays no attention to him; she is intent on a gesture of love and reverence for Jesus. So intent that she does not stop to think how shocked a group of Pharisees would be to see her let down her hair in public and caress the feet of a man. They would see a seductive prostitute, while she experienced only repentance for her past sins and chaste love for Jesus. We are not told how they had first met, but it is clear that she has already repented of her sins and begun a new life before she enters Simon's house. And she has been forgiven, though she may not realize that she has been.

> One of the Pharisees asked Jesus to eat with him, and he went into the Pharisee's house and took his place at the table. And a woman in the city, who was a sinner, having learned that he was eating in the Pharisee's house, brought an alabaster jar of ointment. She stood behind him at his feet, weeping, and began to bathe his feet with her tears and to dry them with her hair. Then she continued kissing his feet and anointing them with the ointment.

> *Luke 7:36-38*

This incident helped Simon to make up his mind about the man he had thought might be a prophet. Simon himself would have flinched from the touch of this woman, and presumed any pious Jew who knew about her would do the same. Actually, Jesus knew more about her than Simon did.

Simon does not express his shock aloud, but Jesus reads his heart and responds to his thoughts with a story.

It is a story about the great love a person who has been forgiven will have. Grudgingly, Simon admits that this is true in principle, though he does not see its connection to the present incident. Jesus then asks Simon, "Do you see this woman?" Jesus sees a holy woman, who has repented her sins, been forgiven, and is now filled with love. Simon does not see this woman; like most of us most of the time, he only sees what she used to be.

Then Jesus turns gently to the humiliated woman and praises her. "Your faith has saved you." She has already been forgiven, but he hopes by this public affirmation of her to restore her to a place of respect in her community.

This story is found only in Luke's Gospel. It is typical of his concern for the poor, for women, for sinners.

Now when the Pharisee who had invited him saw it, he said to himself, "If this man were a prophet, he would have known who and what kind of woman this is who is touching him—that she is a sinner." Jesus spoke up and said to him, "Simon, I have something to say to you." "Teacher," he replied, "speak." "A certain creditor had two debtors; one owed five hundred denarii, and the other fifty. When they could not pay, he canceled the debts for both of them. Now which of them will love him more?" Simon answered, "I suppose the one for whom he canceled the greater debt." And Jesus said to him, "You have judged rightly." Then turning toward the woman, he said to Simon, "Do you see this woman? I entered your house; you gave me no water for my feet, but she has bathed my feet with her tears and dried them with her hair. You gave me no kiss, but from the time I came in she has not stopped kissing my feet. You did not anoint my head with oil, but she has anointed my feet with ointment. Therefore, I tell you, her sins, which were many, have been forgiven; hence she has shown great love. But the one to whom little is forgiven, loves little." Then he said to her, "Your sins are forgiven." But those who were at the table with him began to say among themselves, "Who is this who even forgives sins?" And he said to the woman,

"Your faith has saved you; go in peace."

Luke 7:39-50

As Jesus continued his mission, he was accompanied by two groups who will continue to be important until the end of the story: the twelve apostles and "the women." Both will be important as those who witnessed the events of the public life. The women will be especially important as those who also witnessed the death, burial and empty tomb.

It was common for rabbis to travel around accompanied by disciples. It was unheard of for women to be included among those disciples. It must have caused scandal, as the repentant woman who anointed his feet did. These were women who had been healed by Jesus, perhaps of mental illness. At least "seven demons" signifies some very serious disorder. There is no reason to think that any of them had been prostitutes, though later centuries pictured Mary Magdalene that way. Mary Magdalene and Susanna may have been single women, since their names are not connected to any husband. Perhaps they had been ostracized from society because of their illness. When they were healed by Jesus, they did not return to their former families but formed a new kind of community around him.

These were women with resources, and they showed their gratitude by using them generously in providing for the needs of Jesus and the disciples. Luke is always eager to give his readers examples of the right use of material goods. In the church he knew, women like Tabitha and Lydia served as benefactors to the Christian community. He wanted them to find models in the women who had been benefactors of Jesus himself.

In every list of these women who followed Jesus, Mary Magdalene is mentioned first, as Peter is mentioned first in every list of the apostles. She clearly had a role of leadership among the women. Early Christians would delight in creating stories about her missionary activities after the resurrection.

> Soon afterwards he went on through cities and villages, proclaiming and bringing the good news of the kingdom of God. The twelve were with him, as well as some women who had been cured of evil spirits and infirmities: Mary, called Magdalene, from whom seven demons had gone out, and Joanna, the wife of Herod's steward Chuza, and Susanna, and many others, who provided for them out of their resources.

Luke 8:1-3

Questions for Reflection

1. When did it happen that you, or someone you know, became troubled and doubtful, like John the Baptist, when things did not turn out as you thought God had intended?

2. Who today preaches in the style of John the Baptist? In the style of Jesus?

3. Christians serve God in a variety of styles, as John and Jesus did. What styles of Christian life do you prefer?

4. Jesus tried to open John's eyes to a new vision by a quotation from Isaiah. When has a Scripture passage suggested to you a change in your thinking or actions?

5. Give examples of converted sinners who seem to love Jesus more fervently than Christians who have always been law-abiding.

6. What women in the church today give their lives to following Jesus and providing for those in need?

Suggestions for Further Reading

Matthew 27:56-61; 28:1-10; Mark 16:9;
Luke 23:44-56; 24:1-12; John 20:1-18:
Mary Magdalene

Acts 9:36-42: Tabitha

Acts 16:11-15, 40: Lydia

CHAPTER SIX

Two Daughters, and the Continuing Education of the Disciples

Two Related Stories

THE NEXT TWO STORIES ARE CONNECTED. The story of the daughter of Jairus is like a frame around the story of the woman with hemorrhages. Luke likes to use this technique; it is an indication that he wants his readers to think about the two stories in relation to each other. Both are about "daughters" in desperate need. Both are healed through faith in Jesus. One was twelve years old. The other had been ill for twelve years.

The stories begin with Jairus, a leader of the synagogue, coming to Jesus and falling at his feet. This is very unusual. Jesus was accustomed to hostility from Jewish religious leaders. But Luke does not want us to generalize about any category of people. Jairus has faith. He also has such an intense love for his only daughter that he forgets his position of dignity and humbles himself before the traveling preacher.

Luke likes to show Jesus performing similar miracles for a man and a woman. The raising from the dead of the only daughter of Jairus parallels the raising from the dead of the only son of the widow of Nain.

Now when Jesus returned, the crowd welcomed him, for they were all waiting for him. Just then there came a man named Jairus, a leader of the synagogue. He fell at Jesus' feet and begged him to come to his house, for he had an only daughter, about twelve years old, who was dying.

Luke 8:40–42

As Jesus walks toward the home of this important personage, surrounded by crowds as usual, he suddenly stops and demands to know who has touched him. A strange question! But Jesus is not speaking of merely physical touch. Someone, by way of physical touch, has made real contact with him. He felt power draining from him, as we may when we have poured our energy into a great work.

The woman who had "touched" him in this special way was a woman on in years, who had suffered perpetual bleeding for twelve years. She was not only physically exhausted, but also totally alienated from her community. Jewish law considered such women "unclean," and anyone who had contact with them was contaminated by them. Her acts of joining the crowd and of furtively touching Jesus were shocking violations of law, showing just how desperate she was.

It is therefore not surprising that at first she denies having touched Jesus. It would be a terrible embarrassment in the presence of the leader of the synagogue and all the people of the town to acknowledge what she had done. Only when it becomes clear that Jesus will not continue on his errand until he knows, does she confess, trembling. Jesus relieves her shame by affirming her. It is her faith, he says, that has healed her.

> As he went, the crowds pressed in on him. Now there was a woman who had been suffering from hemorrhages for twelve years; and though she had spent all she had on physicians, no one could cure her. She came up behind him and touched the fringe of his clothes, and immediately her hemorrhage stopped. Then Jesus asked, "Who touched me?" When all denied it, Peter said, "Master, the crowds surround you and press in on you." But Jesus said, "Someone touched me; for I noticed that power had gone out from me." When the woman saw that she could not remain hidden, she came trembling; and falling down before him, she declared in the presence of all the people why she had touched him, and how she had been immediately healed.

He said to her, "Daughter, your faith has made you well; go in peace."

Luke 8:42-48

—⁓—

It seemed that this interruption had cost Jesus the chance to cure Jairus's daughter. The little girl had died. But Jesus urged Jairus, as he sometimes urges us, to have faith even when the situation seemed impossible. He walked through the mourners who were wailing in the style of their culture. He went into the room where the girl's body lay, bringing only his closest friends and the girl's parents with him. Then he touched the corpse, an act that would have made him ritually unclean if his contact with the woman with the hemorrhage had not already done so. He took her by the hand, raised her up, and told her astonished parents to give her something to eat. Later, he himself would ask for something to eat when he rose from the dead. Ghosts do not eat. Eating is a sign of ordinary human life, something that connects us with all other humans.

While he was still speaking, someone came from the leader's house to say, "Your daughter is dead; do not trouble the teacher any longer." When Jesus heard this, he replied, "Do not fear. Only believe, and she will be saved." When he came to the house, he did not allow anyone to enter with him, except Peter, John, and James, and the child's father and mother. They were all weeping and wailing for her; but he said, "Do not weep; for she is not dead but sleeping." And they laughed at him, knowing that she was dead. But he took her by the hand and called out, "Child, get up!" Her spirit returned, and she got up at once. Then he directed them to give her something to eat. Her parents were astounded; but he ordered them to tell no one what had happened.

Luke 8:49-56

—⁓—

Peter's Profession of Faith

Again Luke shows us Jesus at prayer, away from the crowds, but with his disciples around him. He wonders what people are saying about him, and asks the disciples. They repeat some of the rumors they have heard. Then he asks them, and us, the crucial question, "Who do you say I am?" Though the question is addressed to the whole group, Peter answers for them. They have come to realize that Jesus is the "Messiah," the anointed king promised by God.

> Once when Jesus was praying alone, with only the disciples near him, he asked them, "Who do the crowds say that I am?" They answered, "John the Baptist; but others, Elijah; and still others, that one of the ancient prophets has arisen." He said to them, "But who do you say that I am?" Peter answered, "The Messiah of God."

Luke 9:18-20

The Suffering Messiah

The disciples have mastered Lesson One. They know that Jesus is the Messiah. However, it would be dangerous to mention this publicly because the common expectation is that the Messiah will be a warrior king who will free them from the Romans as David freed them from the Philistines. The disciples need to come to a different understanding of what the Messiah is.

Now they are ready for Lesson Two, a much more difficult one. Not only is the Messiah not a warrior, he will be rejected and killed. He will also be raised, but they were probably too shocked at the death part to hear the resurrection part. (At least after Jesus' death they do not seem to remember it.)

The second part of the lesson strikes home even more painfully. It is not only Jesus who must suffer. Suffering is an integral part of Christian life. Anyone who follows Jesus "must" carry a cross, like one condemned to death. Here Luke adds to Mark's version the word "daily." He wants to emphasize that Jesus is not only talking about a dramatic martyrdom at the end of life, but about every day of life.

This section ends with a puzzling sentence: "There are some standing here who will not taste death before they see the kingdom of God." It is not surprising that many early Christians understood from this that the Second Coming of Jesus would be within the lifetime of some of his contemporaries. It is a case where the literal meaning is clearly not the correct one.

> He sternly ordered and commanded them not to tell anyone, saying, "The Son of Man must undergo great suffering, and be rejected by the elders, chief priests, and scribes, and be killed, and on the third day be raised."
>
> Then he said to them all, "If any want to become my followers, let them deny themselves and take up their cross daily and follow me. For those who want to save their life will lose it, and those who lose their life for my sake will save it. What does it profit them if they gain the whole world, but lose or forfeit themselves? Those who are ashamed of me and of my words, of them the Son of Man will be ashamed when he comes in his glory and the glory of the Father and of the holy angels. But truly I tell you, there are some standing here who will not taste death before they see the kingdom of God."

Luke 9:21-27

The Transfiguration

The education of the followers of Jesus continues. The same three, Peter, James and John, who had witnessed the raising of

Jairus' daughter are now to witness something even more wonderful. With Jesus, they climb up a mountain to pray. There, for a moment, they glimpse the true glory of Jesus. It can happen with ordinary human beings, too, that sometimes by a special grace we glimpse for a moment who this person really is.

With the glorified Jesus they see Moses and Elijah, the two Old Testament figures who had climbed Mount Sinai for an experience of God. (On top of Mount Sinai today is a Greek Orthodox chapel with a picture of Jesus, Moses and Elijah at the Transfiguration.) For the Jewish people, they represent the law and the prophets. By talking with them, Jesus is showing the continuity between the Old Testament and the New Testament which he is inaugurating. The three of them discuss his "departure" or "exodus." This word refers backward to the exodus of Israel from Egypt, but also forward to Jesus' death and resurrection, which will be a new exodus. Jesus will lead God's people through the waters of death to new life as Moses had led them through the Red Sea to their birth as a free people. It seems that these wise ancestors of his are preparing Jesus for his death and resurrection.

The disciples appear to be in a daze, halfway between sleeping and waking. They marvel at what they see. Like most human beings at such a peak experience, they want to capture the moment, to somehow hold on to it. The first thing that comes to their heads is to put up a structure, a permanent memorial of the experience. Three structures will be even better, one each for Jesus, Moses and Elijah. They are not called to settle in at this holy place, but to journey on. Nevertheless, if you climb Mount Tabor today, you will find a great church in honor of Jesus' Transfiguration, with little chapels for Moses and Elijah!

Instead of building structures, they were called to enter into a cloud, and they were terrified. Our human nature likes to be busy, but it rebels against the cloud, which represents that presence of God we cannot see or understand, which makes us feel blind and helpless.

It is only in this awesome cloud that they hear God's words, identifying Jesus as God's chosen one.

> Now about eight days after these sayings Jesus took with him Peter and John and James, and went up on the mountain to pray. And while he was praying, the appearance of his face changed, and his clothes became dazzling white. Suddenly they saw two men, Moses and Elijah, talking to him. They appeared in glory and were speaking of his departure, which he was about to accomplish at Jerusalem. Now Peter and his companions were weighed down with sleep; but since they had stayed awake, they saw his glory and the two men who stood with him. Just as they were leaving him, Peter said to Jesus, "Master, it is good for us to be here; let us make three dwellings, one for you, one for Moses, and one for Elijah"—not knowing what he said. While he was saying this, a cloud came and overshadowed them; and they were terrified as they entered the cloud. Then from the cloud came a voice that said, "This is my Son, my Chosen; listen to him!" When the voice had spoken, Jesus was found alone. And they kept silent and in those days told no one any of the things they had seen.

> *Luke 9:28-36*

The Epileptic Boy

The next story brings the disciples brutally down to earth. When they come down from the mountain, they are confronted by a crowd surrounding a frantic father who has brought his epileptic son to be healed by the disciples. The seriousness of the situation is highlighted by a vivid description of the child's symptoms, and by the fact that he is an only child, the father's only hope to remain part of Israel through his descendants. The disciples had been given power over demons (Luke 9:1), but this one was beyond them. Jesus shows his disappointment at how slow they are to learn, his concern about how they will manage when he is gone. Then Jesus heals the poor boy, restoring him to his family.

On the next day, when they had come down from the mountain, a great crowd met him. Just then a man from the crowd shouted, "Teacher, I beg you to look at my son; he is my only child. Suddenly a spirit seizes him, and all at once he shrieks. It convulses him until he foams at the mouth; it mauls him and will scarcely leave him. I begged your disciples to cast it out, but they could not." Jesus answered, "You faithless and perverse generation, how much longer must I be with you and bear with you? Bring your son here." While he was coming, the demon dashed him to the ground in convulsions. But Jesus rebuked the unclean spirit, healed the boy, and gave him back to his father. And all were astounded at the greatness of God.

Luke 9:37-43

The Child as Model

We see another example of the slowness of the disciples to learn Jesus' message when they begin arguing about which of them is the greatest. Jesus shocks them by taking a little child and telling the ambitious disciples that their value system is not his. In their society, a child was at the very bottom of the social ladder. For Jesus' followers, the least in the world's eyes, such as a child, is the greatest.

An argument arose among them as to which one of them was the greatest. But Jesus, aware of their inner thoughts, took a little child and put it by his side, and said to them, "Whoever welcomes this child in my name welcomes me, and whoever welcomes me welcomes the one who sent me; for the least among all of you is the greatest."

Luke 9:46-48

—⁓—

Disciples Without Credentials

The education of the disciples continues, with John, who has just come down from the Transfiguration experience, showing how little he understands Jesus' ways. Jesus' disciples were unable to cast the demon out of the epileptic boy, but other people, not members of their privileged group, are casting out demons in Jesus' name! John is like any of us who are intent on limiting God's actions to our own group, or to what we see as properly approved channels. Jesus, it seems, has followers who are not known to his "in group!"

John answered, "Master, we saw someone casting out demons in your name, and we tried to stop him, because he does not follow with us." But Jesus said to him, "Do not stop him; for whoever is not against you is for you."

Luke 9:49-50

—⁓—

Questions for Reflection

1. Do you think the woman with a hemorrhage was right to violate the law by touching other people? Do you know any case today where a person was justified in violating a law?

2. The disciples only gradually came to see that Jesus was indeed the Messiah, but a very different kind of Messiah from the one they had expected. In your life, has your idea of Jesus changed?

3 Have you had an experience you did not want to move on from, as the disciples did not want to move on from the Transfiguration?

4. When you hear Jesus saying, "The least among you will be the greatest," of whom do you think?

5. Do you know people who, like John, resent the successful ministry of those whom they see as not properly authorized?

6. Do you know of anyone who is not a practicing Christian, yet acts in the spirit of Jesus?

Suggestions for Further Reading
Exodus 24:15-18: Moses

1 Kings 19:8-13: Elijah

CHAPTER SEVEN

Journey Toward Jerusalem

Teaching on the Journey

NOW WE BEGIN THE LONG SECTION OF Luke's Gospel usually called the "Journey Narrative." We can see its importance for Luke, as it occupies almost half of his Gospel, and contains much material found only in his Gospel. The more relaxed ministry in Galilee is over, and Jesus has "set his face to go to Jerusalem." Jerusalem will be the place of his death and resurrection. Now everything is pointing in that direction. Much is happening on the journey, all of it planned to educate the disciples, to prepare them for what is ahead. Sometimes it is when people, such as the terminally ill, are aware of being close to death that they have the most to teach their companions. This seems to be the case with Jesus.

> When the days drew near for [Jesus] to be taken up, he set his face to go to Jerusalem.
>
> *Luke 9:51*

—~~~—

Journey Through Samaria

The journey passes through Samaria. This was not a geographical necessity. While the most direct route from Galilee to Jerusalem was through Samaria, most Jews chose alternate routes in order to avoid passing through a land they detested, and where they were detested. Jews looked on Samaritans as a kind of half-breed and heretical branch of Judaism. As is often the case, hostilities within the family were even greater than those against Gentiles, who were complete outsiders.

The hostility between Jews and Samaritans went back over seven hundred years, to the time when the northern kingdom, Israel, was conquered by the Assyrians. It was the policy of the Assyrians to send most of the population of any place they conquered into another country, so there would not be any possibility of rebellion. The poorer, less educated Israelites remained, but had to live mingled with people of other nationalities imported by the Assyrians.

Because most ancient people believed there were many gods, each in charge of a particular territory, the immigrants wanted to worship the god of Israel. They did the best they could without learned priests to instruct them fully, but the Jews considered the Samaritan theology less than orthodox. And the Jews, who put great value on their pure bloodline, were contemptuous of the Samaritans, who were the product of intermarriage between the remnant of Israelites and the foreigners imported by the Assyrians.

The disciples were probably surprised when Jesus decided to travel through Samaria, and the messengers he sent ahead to make arrangements for accommodations were probably not too happy with the job. They were hardly surprised that, as with many countries and hotels through the ages, the Samaritans refused them hospitality because they were Jews.

James and John were special friends of Jesus. With Peter, they had been the only witnesses of the Transfiguration. They had heard Jesus' instructions about what to do when you are rejected. "Wherever they do not welcome you, as you are leaving that town shake the dust off your feet as a testimony against them" (Luke 9:5). Yet their reaction is far from Jesus' nonviolent way. Like some Christians today, they imagine their violence is in defense of Jesus, but do not see how contrary it is to the spirit of Jesus.

Rejection is to be expected in Christian life. Luke begins his great travel narrative with the rejection of Jesus because he is a Jew. He will end it with the rejection of Jesus by the Jews and Romans, which led to his death.

> And he sent messengers ahead of him. On their way they entered a village of the Samaritans to make ready for him, but they did not receive him, because his face was set toward Jerusalem. When his disciples James and John saw it, they said, "Lord, do you want us to command fire to come down from heaven and consume them?" But he turned and rebuked them. Then they went on to another village.

Luke 9:52-56

Some Who Wish to Follow Jesus

When the Samaritans refused him hospitality, Jesus must have become more aware than ever that he was now a homeless transient. He reminds the volunteer who asks to follow him (the Greek text does not indicate whether it was a man or a woman) of his homelessness. He invites two others to follow him. It seems that they want to respond, but they ask for delays, for what appear to be good reasons. The first wants to bury a father, a very serious obligation in that culture. (Presumably, the father was living, and this involved caring for him until he died.) The next only wanted to say farewell to family. But the call is urgent; Jesus allows no delays. Do these three become disciples? We are never told, perhaps because we are supposed to see them as representatives of ourselves. Will we follow Jesus in spite of the difficulties involved? Only we readers can answer the question.

> As they were going along the road, someone said to him, "I will follow you wherever you go." And Jesus said to him, "Foxes have holes, and birds of the air have nests; but the Son of Man has nowhere to lay his head." To another he said, "Follow me." But he said, "Lord, first let me go and bury

my father." But Jesus said to him, "Let the dead bury their own dead; but as for you, go and proclaim the kingdom of God." Another said, "I will follow you, Lord; but let me first say farewell to those at my home." Jesus said to him, "No one who puts a hand to the plow and looks back is fit for the kingdom of God."

Luke 9:57–62

Martha and Mary

The next stop on the journey to Jerusalem is the home of Martha and Mary. Only Luke gives us this famous story. Martha is the chief character in the story. It begins and ends with her, and takes place in her home. She is presumably the elder sister, the head of the household. She welcomes Jesus and his disciples into her home. Since she has no telephone or e-mail, she had no opportunity to prepare food for her guests in advance, so she rushes around frantically trying to get a suitable meal ready. Much as she wants Jesus to spend time in her home, she feels upset and overworked. What makes matters worse is that she also feels abandoned. Her younger sister, who should be helping, is just sitting at Jesus' feet, being no help whatever.

To sit at the feet of a teacher is to be a disciple. Mary was behaving like a disciple. This was shocking behavior; it was unheard of for a teacher to have a woman as disciple. But Jesus does not seem to care about the proprieties. He is a teacher, and he appreciates a good student. He welcomes her as a disciple.

Martha, distraught with her domestic concerns, complains to Jesus about all the work with which Mary is not helping. She is the type of hostess who spares no efforts to provide a grand meal, but forgets that the one thing necessary in hospitality is to pay attention to the guest. Instead, she violates the rules of hospitality by involving her guest in an unpleasant family conflict. Jesus does not criticize her for preparing the meal, which he will soon enjoy, but for not respecting the fact that at that moment Mary is called to a different kind of service. Work is good, but it is not the whole of Christian life.

Mary is a reminder to us that we need time simply sitting at the feet of Jesus. Mary is a reminder to us that good works like preparing a meal for Jesus can be spoiled by self-pity and criticism of others.

> Now as they went on their way, he entered a certain village, where a woman named Martha welcomed him into her home. She had a sister named Mary, who sat at the Lord's feet and listened to what he was saying. But Martha was distracted by her many tasks, so she came to him and asked, "Lord, do you not care that my sister has left me to do all the work by myself? Tell her then to help me." But the Lord answered her, "Martha, Martha, you are worried and distracted by many things; there is need of only one thing. Mary has chosen the better part, which will not be taken away from her."

Luke 10:38–42

Teachings on Prayer

Jesus took time for prayer on his journey. In prayer he was in contact with the deepest reality of who he was, his relationship with his Father. The disciples noticed the intensity of his prayer, and wished they could pray like that. So one of them asked him to teach them to pray. Many complicated books have since been written about how to pray, but Jesus gave only a simple formula. Luke's version is even shorter than Matthew's, which is the familiar version used by the church. The basic pattern is clear. First, we are to reach up to God, trying to share God's great concern for the kingdom. After that, we are to lift up to God the needs we see in our small world. This is not just a formula for occasional use, but also a guide for all prayer.

He was praying in a certain place, and after he had fin-
ished, one of his disciples said to him, "Lord, teach us to
pray, as John taught his disciples." He said to them, "When
you pray, say:
Father, hallowed be your name.
Your kingdom come.
Give us each day our daily bread.
And forgive us our sins,
    for we ourselves forgive everyone indebted to us.
And do not bring us to the time of trial."

Luke 11:1-4

Jesus continues to teach about the prayer of petition. Only
Luke, who has a special interest in prayer, tells the parable of
the person who receives a guest at midnight and has no food
to offer the guest. In a culture that prized hospitality, this was
an emergency. He goes to a neighbor to beg for bread, but
gets it only by persistence. The message is that we are to be
persistent in bringing our needs to God.

Then we are told clearly that everyone who asks will
receive. Notice, we are not promised that we will receive
what we ask for. God may see that what we ask for is not
really what we need. But it would be absurd to think that
what God gives is bad. Even human parents give only good
things to their children.

Matthew has this passage, but where he says God will
give "good things" to those who pray, Luke says specifically
that God will give "the Holy Spirit." Luke has a special interest in the Holy Spirit; only he will tell the story of
Pentecost.

And he said to them, "Suppose one of you has a friend,
and you go to him at midnight and say to him, 'Friend, lend
me three loaves of bread; for a friend of mine has arrived,
and I have nothing to set before him.' And he answers from

within, 'Do not bother me; the door has already been locked, and my children are with me in bed; I cannot get up and give you anything.' I tell you, even though he will not get up and give him anything because he is his friend, at least because of his persistence he will get up and give him whatever he needs.

"So I say to you, Ask, and it will be given you; search, and you will find; knock, and the door will be opened for you. For everyone who asks receives, and everyone who searches finds, and for everyone who knocks, the door will be opened. Is there anyone among you who, if your child asks for a fish, will give a snake instead of a fish? Or if the child asks for an egg, will give a scorpion? If you then, who are evil, know how to give good gifts to your children, how much more will the heavenly Father give the Holy Spirit to those who ask him!"

Luke 11:5-13

The Blessed Mother

A woman in the crowd calls out her admiration for Jesus by saying "Blessed is the womb that bore you..." This is true enough, but Jesus does not accept this praise which seems to be based on the assumption by his culture that a woman's only value is in childbearing. He does not deny his mother's blessedness, but tells us that it comes from the fact that she hears the word of God and obeys it. Luke has already shown us Mary as one who in a preeminent way hears the word of God and obeys it (Luke 1:45; 2:19, 51).

> While he was saying this, a woman in the crowd raised her voice and said to him, "Blessed is the womb that bore you, and the breasts that nursed you!" But he said, "Blessed rather are those who hear the word of God and obey it!"

Luke 11:27, 28

The Danger of Riches

The death of parents can lead to terrible family squabbles about inheritance. A man who felt he had been cheated in such a situation came to Jesus to settle the problem, as Martha had come to him with her complaint about Mary. It was common for rabbis to be called on for such decisions. Jesus refuses to serve as arbitrator, but he uses the situation as a starting point for a serious teaching. "Be on your guard against all kinds of greed..." He sees beneath the legal debate the deeper issue, greed. The person blinded by greed imagines that abundance of possessions gives life, but that is not true. Jesus illustrates his point with a parable, one to be found only in Luke. Some people in Luke's community must have been wealthy, because he emphasizes the proper use of wealth, and warns often about its dangers.

The story reminds us of Lazarus and the rich man, another parable found only in Luke. This one is about a rich man with a good problem: he has so many possessions he has no room to store them all. And he must store them, as it does not enter his head to share them with those who have nothing. Once he solves this little problem, he feels he will be in control. He can safely retire, with IRAs to see him through a comfortable life. But in reality he is a fool. The security that comes from possessions is an illusion.

Someone in the crowd said to him, "Teacher, tell my brother to divide the family inheritance with me." But he said to him, "Friend, who set me to be a judge or arbitrator over you?" And he said to them, "Take care! Be on your guard against all kinds of greed, for one's life does not consist in the abundance of possessions." Then he told them a parable. "The land of a rich man produced abundantly. And he thought to himself, 'What should I do, for I have no place to store my crops?' Then he said, 'I will do this: I will pull down my barns and build larger ones, and there I will store all my grain and my goods. And I will say to my soul, 'Soul, you have ample goods laid up for many years; relax, eat, drink, be merry.' But God said to him, 'You fool! This very night your life is being demanded of you. And the things you have prepared, whose will they be?' So it is with those who store up treasures for themselves but are not rich toward God."

Luke 12:13-21

Jesus continues his teaching about the goods of this world. We are not to worry about our material needs. Those who do not know God strive for these things, but Christians strive that God will truly rule over their own lives and their world. They do not have to worry about their real needs, because God knows about them and will provide. Worry is a great hindrance to the wholehearted service of God, an unconscious denial of the power and goodness of God.

To illustrate his point, Jesus points to the ravens and the wildflowers. How beautifully God provides for them! Jesus could learn about God by observing even the littlest part of God's creation, and he is teaching us to do the same.

He said to his disciples, "Therefore I tell you, do not worry about your life, what you will eat, or about your body, what you will wear. For life is more than food, and the body more than clothing. Consider the ravens: they neither sow nor reap, they have neither storehouse nor barn, and yet God feeds them. Of how much more value are you than the birds! And can any of you by worrying add a single hour to your span of life?" If then you are not able to do so small a thing as that, why do you worry about the rest? Consider the lilies, how they grow: they neither toil nor spin; yet I tell you, even Solomon in all his glory was not clothed like one of these. But if God so clothes the grass of the field, which is alive today and tomorrow is thrown into the oven, how much more will he clothe you—you of little faith! And do not keep striving for what you are to eat and what you are to drink, and do not keep worrying. For it is the nations of the world that strive after all these things, and your Father knows that you need them. Instead, strive for his kingdom, and these things will be given to you as well."

Luke 12:22-31

The Christian who is freed from worry about material things will be able to use those things in the way God intends, by sharing with the poor. This leads to the true security, treasure in heaven which death does not take away.

Do not be afraid, little flock, for it is your Father's good pleasure to give you the kingdom. Sell your possessions, and give alms. Make purses for yourselves that do not wear out, an unfailing treasure in heaven, where no thief comes near and no moth destroys. For where your treasure is, there your heart will be also.

Luke 12:32-34

Questions for Reflection

1. Have you ever felt rejected because you were not part of some "in group," as Jesus and the disciples were rejected by the Samaritans? Have you ever been part of an "in group" that rejected others?

2. Is there something you feel the Lord is calling you to that you are putting off because of something you want to do first, like those called in Luke 9:59-62 who wanted first to bury a parent or say farewell to family?

3. Are you more like Martha or Mary? How do you feel about being whichever you are?

4. What of Jesus' teaching on prayer in 11:1-13 is most helpful for you?

5. What story about people today do you know that has the same message as Jesus' story of the rich fool?

6. Jesus noticed the wildflowers, and got a message from them. What in nature has a spiritual message for you?

7. What is most helpful to you in your effort not to worry about material things?

Suggestions for Further Reading

> 2 Kings 17:24-41: Origin of the Samaritans
>
> Luke 10:25-37: The Good Samaritan
>
> John 4:1-42: Jesus and the Samaritan Woman
>
> Acts 8:4-25: The Conversion of the Samaritans
>
> John 11:1-57; 12:1-8: Martha and Mary in John's Gospel

CHAPTER EIGHT

On the Journey

A Glimpse Ahead

AS JESUS AND THE DISCIPLES JOURNEY toward Jerusalem, he usually appears as a calm and capable teacher, instructing them about how his followers are to live. But a moment comes when he reveals his own inner struggle, and the future that overshadows this whole journey to Jerusalem. The future for which he yearns intensely is Pentecost, the holy fire that will empower these weak disciples and through them transform the earth. Perhaps Jesus is remembering that at the beginning of his ministry, John the Baptist had prophesied that he would "baptize with the Holy Spirit and with fire" (Luke 3:16). But he knows that before Pentecost must come his own "baptism," the cross. As the early Christians went down into a baptismal pool and were immersed before coming out of it, Jesus had to be plunged into his passion and death before his resurrection (cf. Mark 10:38). In fact, the word "baptism," before it was applied to the sacrament, simply meant "immersion." In these verses we get a rare glimpse of the stress beneath Jesus' usual calm, of the urgency he feels about this journey to Jerusalem.

I came to bring fire to the earth, and how I wish it were already kindled! I have a baptism with which to be baptized, and what stress I am under until it is completed!

Luke 12:49-50

Jesus Divides Families

Perhaps Jesus revealed his own pain in order to prepare the disciples for his next words, which predict one of the sharpest pains of discipleship. At Jesus' birth the angels sang about peace on earth, and Gabriel promised Zechariah that his son John would turn the hearts of fathers to their sons (Luke 1:17). But what Jesus' disciples actually experience will not be all peace. In fact, they are often deprived of peace in exactly the place where they most expect to find it, their own homes.

Family unity was an extremely high value in the society in which Jesus lived. Since the sexes did not mix much in their daily social lives, the most important relationships were those between fathers and sons and those between mothers, or mothers-in-law, and daughters. (The son ordinarily remained permanently in the home of his father, but the daughter at her marriage moved from the home of her mother to that of her mother-in-law, so the son did not have the close daily relationship with his father-in-law that the daughter had with her mother-in-law.) For people for whom family values were the primary values, these relationships were supremely important. But Jesus' coming will bring division even within the household. Perhaps as Jesus anticipates the pain his disciples will endure, he is also remembering his own pain when his extended family turned against him (Mark 3:21; 31–34; John 7:3–5).

> Do you think that I have come to bring peace to the earth? No, I tell you, but rather division! From now on five in one household will be divided, three against two and two against three; they will be divided:
> father against son
>   and son against father,
> mother against daughter
>   and daughter against mother,

> mother-in-law against her daughter-in-law
> and daughter-in-law against mother-in-law.

Luke 12:51–53

—~~~—

A Woman Is Cured on the Sabbath

Jesus just spoke about the personal relationships of men and of women. Now he will cure a woman and a man in parallel encounters, both on the Sabbath.

The woman is pathetic. She is crippled by a spirit, as so many women today are crippled by a poor self-image. She is so bent over she cannot see the stars; she cannot look another person in the eye. She is alone, without any family to give her love or dignity. She lives on the margins of society, socially invisible, as the handicapped so often are. It does not occur to her that, at her age, she could be cured of an ailment that has dominated her life for eighteen years. She can hardly see Jesus from her bent-over position, and she would never have the courage to speak to him. But Jesus sees her, as others do not. He calls her from her place on the margins to come to him. And, shocking the bystanders, he even touches her. For the first time in eighteen years, this woman stands up straight. She becomes a liberated woman.

> Now he was teaching in one of the synagogues on the sabbath. And just then there appeared a woman with a spirit that had crippled her for eighteen years. She was bent over and was quite unable to stand up straight. When Jesus saw her, he called her over and said, "Woman, you are set free from your ailment." When he laid his hands on her, immediately she stood up straight and began praising God.

Luke 13:10–13

—~~~—

Now we see an example of the divisions that Jesus causes. The woman praises God and the crowd of common people rejoices. But the leader of the synagogue is indignant because this cure has violated the rules he teaches. Perhaps he feels his position of religious authority is threatened by this upstart Jesus. Yet he does not speak directly to Jesus who threatens him; he addresses his indignation to the crowd. Jesus is not so devious. He responds directly to his opponent, arguing in rabbinic style that if an animal can be unbound to bring it to water on the Sabbath, a woman can be unbound from the chains of Satan on the Sabbath. And he describes the woman in a way that shows she is no longer alone; she is of the family of Abraham. Scripture often speaks of the sons of Abraham, but only Jesus notices that Abraham has daughters also.

> But the leader of the synagogue, indignant because Jesus had cured on the sabbath, kept saying to the crowd, "There are six days on which work ought to be done; come on those days and be cured, and not on the sabbath day." But the Lord answered him and said, "You hypocrites! Does not each of you on the sabbath untie his ox or his donkey from the manger, and lead it away to give it water? And ought not this woman, a daughter of Abraham whom Satan bound for eighteen long years, be set free from this bondage on the sabbath day?" When he said this, all his opponents were put to shame; and the entire crowd was rejoicing at all the wonderful things that he was doing.

Luke 13:14-17

A Man Is Cured on the Sabbath

In a similar incident on another Sabbath, Jesus cures a man with dropsy, a condition usually described today as generalized edema. The whole body swells because of an excess of fluid, often caused by heart or kidney disease.

In this case, the cure does not occur in the synagogue but at the Sabbath meal that followed the synagogue service. Since this was a traditional time for hospitality, a Pharisee had invited Jesus to the meal. Jesus must have known that the Pharisees would be watching him closely in a hostile way, yet he accepted the invitation. He never gave up on the Pharisees.

When Jesus noticed the man with dropsy he invited the Pharisees to dialogue, asking them if it was permissible to heal on the Sabbath. They refused the invitation. So Jesus healed the man, and then explained his reason in much the same way he had explained his healing of the woman bent over. Again, it is he who speaks directly; the Pharisees will not come out openly with what they think. It can happen with us, too, that by refusing to bring our thoughts into the open we try to prevent Jesus from changing us.

> On one occasion when Jesus was going to the house of a leader of the Pharisees to eat a meal on the sabbath, they were watching him closely. Just then, in front of him, there was a man who had dropsy. And Jesus asked the lawyers and Pharisees, "Is it lawful to cure people on the sabbath, or not?" But they were silent. So Jesus took him and healed him, and sent him away. Then he said to them, "If one of you has a child or an ox that has fallen into a well, will you not immediately pull it out on a sabbath day?" And they could not reply to this.

Luke 14:1-6

The Lost Is Found

Chapter 15 of Luke contains three parables about the lost being found. It is important to notice the double audience to whom these parables are addressed. There are the "lost," the tax collectors and sinners who were the outcasts from respectable Jewish society. They draw near to Jesus, eager to listen to him. But, as in every Sunday service, not all those physically present are listening in that way. On the margins of the scene are the Pharisees and scribes who are listening in their usual hostile way and grumbling because Jesus eats with sinners. Like their ancestors in the desert, they grumble among themselves, but do not speak directly to God, or to Jesus. Jesus, however, addresses them directly with three stories clearly aimed against their self-righteousness.

> Now all the tax collectors and sinners were coming near to listen to him. And the Pharisees and the scribes were grumbling and saying, "This fellow welcomes sinners and eats with them."

Luke 15:1-2

The first parable shows God as a shepherd who has lost one of his sheep. He searches for the lost sheep in the wilderness until he finds it. When at last he finds the sheep he rejoices so much that he has to call in his friends and neighbors to rejoice with him. Notice how often words connected with joy occur in these three stories. This is a major theme of Luke. The message is about the joy that God feels at the return of a sinner.

> So he told them this parable: "Which one of you, having a hundred sheep and losing one of them, does not leave the ninety-nine in the wilderness and go after the one that is lost until he finds it? When he has found it, he lays it on his shoulders and rejoices. And when he comes home, he calls together his friends and neighbors, saying to them, 'Rejoice with me, for I have found my sheep that was lost.' Just so, I tell you, there will be more joy in heaven over one sinner who repents than over ninety-nine righteous persons who need no repentance.

Luke 15:3-7

The second parable shows God as a woman who has lost one of her ten coins. She searches the house diligently until she finds it. Then she rejoices so much that she has to call in her friends and neighbors to rejoice with her. (In a society where men and women live separate social lives, it is taken for granted that the "friends and neighbors" of the shepherd are men; those of the woman are women.) Again, the joy shared by these women is said to be like God's joy in the return of a sinner. While the image of God as shepherd was common-place in Scripture, the image of God as a woman who has lost a coin must have been shocking to Jesus' audience. But it fits with his practice of paralleling a passage about a man with one about a woman. In this case, he gives an image of God as a man, then as a woman.

> Or what woman having ten silver coins, if she loses one of them, does not light a lamp, sweep the house, and search carefully until she finds it? When she has found it, she calls together her friends and neighbors, saying, "Rejoice with me, for I have found the coin that I had lost." Just so, I tell you, there is joy in the presence of the angels of God over one sinner who repents.

Luke 15:8-10

The third parable follows the same basic pattern: God loses something, searches or longs for it, finds it, rejoices at the return and celebrates with a party. However, this story is more developed. It uses Jesus' favorite image of God, that of a father. This father has two sons, who correspond to the two parts of Jesus' audience. He loves both his sons deeply, but neither of them appreciates that love. It is a family story that could happen today.

The younger son is like the "lost" in Jesus' audience. He does not have the decency to wait until his father's death to receive his part of the family inheritance, but demands it while his father is still living. He then cuts his ties with his family and leaves the family home for a distant land, where he wastes his precious heritage. Not only his material heritage, but also his spiritual. No observant Jew would accept a job feeding pigs.

Famine comes on the land, as happens so often today in poor countries. Calamity brings him to his senses and he decides to return home. His loving father has been longing for his return, but the son does not realize that. He expects to be received back only as a servant. To his amazement, his father welcomes him back with extravagant generosity. There is no scolding, no testing. The father even makes an undignified spectacle of himself by pulling up his robes and running to meet the son whom he spies as he approaches. He brings expensive gifts and throws a great party. The characters in the first two stories invited their friends and neighbors to celebrate. By killing the fatted calf, an animal too large for one family to consume, the father makes clear that he will invite the entire village to his celebration.

Then Jesus said, "There was a man who had two sons. The younger of them said to his father, 'Father, give me the share of the property that will belong to me.' So he divided his property between them. A few days later the younger son gathered all he had and traveled to a distant country, and there he squandered his property in dissolute living. When he had spent everything, a severe famine took place throughout that country, and he began to be in need. So he went and hired himself out to one of the citizens of that country, who sent him to his fields to feed the pigs. He would gladly have filled himself with the pods that the pigs were eating; and no one gave him anything. But when he came to himself he said, 'How many of my father's hired hands have bread enough and to spare, but here I am dying of hunger! I will get up and go to my father, and I will say to him, "Father, I have sinned against heaven and before you; I am no longer worthy to be called your son; treat me like one of your hired hands." ' So he set off and went to his father. But while he was still far off, his father saw him and was filled with compassion; he ran and put his arms around him and kissed him. Then the son said to him, 'Father, I have sinned against heaven and before you; I am no longer worthy to be called your son.' But the father said to his slaves, 'Quickly, bring out a robe—the best one—and put it on him; put a ring on his finger and sandals on his feet. And get the fatted calf and kill it, and let us eat and celebrate; for this son of mine was dead and is alive again; he was lost and is found!' And they began to celebrate.

Luke 15:11-24

The second part of the story, the part that has no parallel in the stories of the lost sheep and lost coin, is about the elder brother. The elder brother is like the scribes and Pharisees in Jesus' audience, resentful that Jesus eats with sinners. The father loves both his sons. He shows his love in the beginning by allowing them both the freedom to choose their own paths. Both sons are selfish. The younger takes his inheritance and leaves. The older, who receives the larger portion of the inheritance, stays in his father's house, but he stays there like a slave, obeying his father's orders, but without love. Neither son realizes how much the father loves him.

When the younger son returns, the father in his joy orders a great celebration. The older son, who has been away working, returns to find the celebration in full swing. He is jealous and sullen, a great contrast to the joyous party going on in the house. He refuses to come in to join the celebration. This is a grave insult to the father. Yet the father comes out to him, as he had come out to the returning younger son. As the father sacrificed his dignity to run out to meet the lost son, he sacrifices it to plead with the elder son to join the celebration. It is then that the heart of the elder son is laid bare. He does not address his father respectfully as "Father" but just pours out his anger at both his father and his brother. He never refers to "my brother," only to "this son of yours." He cannot acknowledge those sacred relationships, but his father gently reminds him, calling him "Son" and speaking of "this brother of yours." We do not hear about the elder son's final response. Jesus leaves it to the Pharisees in his audience, and to us readers of the Gospel, to decide how we will respond to the invitation to join in the party celebrating the return of the lost brother. Especially in our later years, we are often called to affirm and celebrate the good things in the lives of younger people. At times we may not feel like going to the party.

> Now his elder son was in the field; and when he came and approached the house, he heard music and dancing. He called one of the slaves and asked what was going on. He replied, "Your brother has come, and your father has killed the fatted calf, because he has got him back safe and sound." Then he became angry and refused to go in. His father came out and began to plead with him. But he answered his father, "Listen! For all these years I have been working like a slave for you, and I have never disobeyed your command; yet you have never given me even a young goat so that I might celebrate with my friends. But when this son of yours came back, who has devoured your property with prostitutes, you killed the fatted calf for him!" Then the father said to him, "Son, you are always with me, and all that is mine is yours. But we had to celebrate and rejoice, because this brother of yours was dead and has come to life; he was lost and has been found."

Luke 15:25-32

This is a story about the unique personal love of God for each of us, the obviously sinful runaway and the even harder-to-love self righteous, joyless slave/son. The father reaches out to both to initiate reconciliation.

Questions for Reflection

1. When have you seen legalism like that of the Pharisees who criticized Jesus for healing on the Sabbath?

2. What situation do you know of where the following of Jesus has caused division in a family or other group?

3. Recall a time when you lost something very precious, searched for it, and found it. What feelings did you have? Can you imagine God having such feelings?

4. Do you think the elder brother joined the party? Why?

5. The Pharisees wanted to exclude sinners and tax collectors. The elder son wanted to exclude his sinful younger brother. Whom do Christians today want to exclude?

6. Which of the three "lost and found" stories do you like best? Why?

Suggestion for Further Reading

Read the full account of the "Travel Narrative" in Luke 9:51–19:27. Notice how the journey toward Jerusalem provides the setting for many familiar passages.

CHAPTER NINE

Riches and Poverty

The Rich Man and Lazarus

LUKE LIKES TO SHOW HOW GOD REVERSES human laws. He tells us that during her pregnancy Mary sang, "God has thrown down the rulers from their thrones, but lifted up the lowly; the hungry he has filled with good things; the rich he has sent away empty" (Luke 1:52, 53). Luke also reports that Jesus pronounced four beatitudes for the poor and a corresponding four woes for the rich. He said, for instance, "Blessed are you who are now hungry, for you will be satisfied" (Luke 6:21), and "Woe to you who are filled now, for you will be hungry" (Luke 6:25).

In the parable of the rich man and Lazarus, Jesus illustrates the same message of how God turns human expectations upside down. There are two main characters in the story. There is a rich man. We know he is rich because he has banquets every day. (Many people of poor nations would describe Americans in the same way.) Also, he is always dressed in expensive imported linen and purple, which even ordinarily wealthy people would wear only for special occasions. This is all we know about him. We do not know if he said his prayers regularly or if he cheated at business. We do not even know his name.

The second character is a beggar who lay outside the gate of the rich man's fine home. He was covered with sores, which probably cut him off from Jewish society as "unclean." He is so hungry that he longs for the chunks of bread which the rich man's guests used to wipe their hands clean after eating a meal with their fingers. These discarded "napkins" were thrown on the floor, where the dogs disposed of them. But none were given to the beggar. His only companions were the dogs who licked his sores. To hear the story as Jesus intended it we have to forget our fondness for pet dogs. The Jews did not domesticate dogs. Dogs were impure animals, scavengers, wild and frightening. The beggar had neither companionship nor wealth nor food nor health. We do not know whether he said his prayers regularly or whether he obeyed the laws. But he had one thing the rich man does not have in the story: he had a name, Lazarus. He is the only character in Jesus' parables who has a name. Perhaps Jesus is challenging us not to generalize about "the poor." Perhaps he wants us to ask ourselves, "What poor people do we know by name?"

To hear the story as Jesus' audience heard it, we have to remember that, for them, wealth was a sign of God's blessing. To be poor was to be cursed, probably through one's own fault, or at least the fault of one's parents. Jesus was turning their theology upside down.

> There was a rich man who was dressed in purple and fine linen and who feasted sumptuously every day. And at his gate lay a poor man named Lazarus, covered with sores, who longed to satisfy his hunger with what fell from the rich man's table; even the dogs would come and lick his sores. . . .

Luke 16:19-20

Now that the two contrasting characters have been introduced, the action of the story begins. Both the rich man and Lazarus die. Death is not the end of this story but its beginning. The rich man, as we would expect, was buried, no doubt with proper ritual in an expensive tomb. We are not told that the poor man was buried. Perhaps there was no ceremony about his death on this earth. Proper burial was a great value in the society of Jesus' time. Not to have it was the final disgrace that could happen to anyone. Lazarus, as far as we know, did not have a crowd of people escorting his body to the tomb, but he was not alone at his death. We are told that the angels carried him away to be with Abraham. We remember this story at funerals when we pray that the angels will lead our departed into paradise. We proclaim that our departed loved ones, like Lazarus, are not alone, but in the company of the angels and Abraham and all the other people of faith who have gone before us.

After death, everything is reversed. The rich man, who is accustomed to looking down on Lazarus lying at his doorstep, is thrown down into Hades. From there he looks up at Abraham far above and Lazarus at Abraham's side. But he hasn't caught on to his new situation. He has always thought of himself as a respectable Jew, so he addresses Abraham as "Father," secure in that privileged relationship. Abraham does not deny the relationship: He replies to him as "Son." But he makes clear that that relationship cannot help the formerly rich man now. The formerly rich man asks "Father Abraham" to send Lazarus to relieve his thirst with a drop of water. He still imagines that Lazarus is a nobody, available as errand boy at his request. It would be beneath his dignity to speak to Lazarus; he asks Abraham to send Lazarus. Abraham responds by reminding him of the contrast between him and Lazarus before death, which corresponds in reverse to their present situation. The chasm that now separates them cannot be crossed. The poor man who lay outside the gate of the rich man's fine house is now inside Abraham's bosom; the rich man is cast outside.

The poor man died and was carried away by the angels to be with Abraham. The rich man also died and was buried. In Hades, where he was being tormented, he looked up and saw Abraham far away with Lazarus by his side. He called out, "Father Abraham, have mercy on me, and send Lazarus to dip the tip of his finger in water and cool my tongue; for I am in agony in these flames." But Abraham said, "Child, remember that during your lifetime you received your good things, and Lazarus in like manner evil things; but now he is comforted here, and you are in agony. Besides all this, between you and us a great chasm has been fixed, so that those who might want to pass from here to you cannot do so, and no one can cross from there to us."

Luke 16:22-26

The formerly rich man had no concern for the poor, but he did have family loyalty. He begged Abraham to send Lazarus, still the errand boy, to warn his five brothers about the fate that awaited them if they continued their present lifestyle. Abraham replied that they have the Scriptures to warn them. The formerly rich man, who had ignored the teaching of the Scripture about concern for the poor all his life, claimed that his brothers would behave differently if they received a special revelation from beyond the grave. But Abraham knew differently. It is not through special revelations that people can be saved but through obedience to God's word which is given to everyone.

He said, "Then, father, I beg you to send him to my father's house—for I have five brothers—that he may warn them, so that they will not also come into this place of torment." Abraham replied, "They have Moses and the prophets; they should listen to them." He said, "No, father Abraham; but if someone goes to them from the dead, they will repent." He said to him, "If they do not listen to Moses and the prophets, neither will they be convinced even if someone rises from the dead."

Luke 16:27-31

The Wealthy Ruler

Another time Jesus is approached by a wealthy ruler. In Matthew this becomes the story of the "rich young man," but Mark gives no hint that he was rich and Luke specifies that he was a "ruler," which strongly implies that he was of mature years. So we should not read Luke's version of this story as directed particularly to the young.

The wealthy ruler comes to Jesus with a real question. This does not sound like the trick questions the Pharisees are always asking him, just to outwit him. It is a question every sincere Christian often asks. "What must I do...?" Jesus gives the standard answer any religious leader of his day would have given: obey the commandments. When we feel the yearning to do great things for God, we have to look first to be sure we are fulfilling our basic responsibilities in life. The wealthy ruler passed the first test. His conscience was clear. Yet he wanted to do more.

Only when this was clear did Jesus respond with his radical demand. "Sell *all* that you have and give to the poor ...and come follow me." This went beyond the many exhortations in the Hebrew Scriptures to give to the poor. It was a call to *become* poor, addressed to a mature man of wealth and status. This man was a seeker, but he was not ready for the answer he received. He had too much to lose. The story only specifies money, but power and status and security and much more come with money. The story can apply to any kind of possession that prevents us from depending completely on God. In one way or other we are probably all possessed by our possessions.

The challenge was too much for the rich man. He became very sad. When Jesus saw the pain on his face he too felt sad and exclaimed, "How hard it is for those who have wealth to enter the kingdom of heaven! It is easier for a camel to pass through the eye of a needle..." The disciples recognized the hyperbole as such; they didn't ask about the size of the needle or the camel. But they also recognized the message and were profoundly shocked by it. Like many Christians today, Jews of Jesus' time usually thought of wealth as a sign of God's favor, poverty as a punishment from God. Yet Jesus told them wealth was a great hindrance to the spiritual life. After two thousand years of Christianity, his statement continues to shock.

A certain ruler asked him, "Good Teacher, what must I do to inherit eternal life?" Jesus said to him, "Why do you call me good? No one is good but God alone. You know the commandments: 'You shall not commit adultery; You shall not murder; You shall not steal; You shall not bear false witness; Honor your father and mother.'" He replied, "I have kept all these since my youth." When Jesus heard this, he said to him, "There is still one thing lacking. Sell all that you own and distribute the money to the poor, and you will have treasure in heaven; then come, follow me." But when he heard this, he became sad; for he was very rich. Jesus looked at him and said, "How hard it is for those who have wealth to enter the kingdom of God! Indeed, it is easier for a camel to go through the eye of a needle than for someone who is rich to enter the kingdom of God."

Those who heard it said, "Then who can be saved?" He replied, "What is impossible for mortals is possible for God."

Luke 18:18-27

The Judge and the Widow

In the next parable, like that of Lazarus and the rich man, there are two characters. The first is a judge. He held a position of great honor and power. Everyone looked up to him. But he was not worthy of his position; he respected neither God nor human beings.

The second character is at the opposite end of the power continuum. She is a widow, a person without power or position to gain respect in her society. Widows through-out Scripture are models of poverty and helplessness. A woman gained what position she could have in biblical times through her husband. Without him, she was of no account at all. She had no real place in the world. For that very reason, Scripture is full of exhortations to care for the widow.

The story is full of humor. This was not your typical quiet, subservient widow. I imagine her as a lively bag lady. She went to the judge to get what she believed she was entitled to. The fact that she went herself indicated that she had no male relative to handle her affairs, as would usually happen. It also indicated that she was a woman of great courage. She believed she was being taken advantage of, and she would not tolerate injustice passively. She not only went to the judge, she kept on going. He clearly cared not at all for her dilemma, but she would not let him forget it. So the woman who appeared to be quite helpless made such a nuisance of herself that the judge finally gave her what was owed her just to be rid of her. He had no fear of God, but he feared that her perpetual nagging would wear him out.

The main message of the story is that we are to be per-sistent in prayer. When we feel helpless and discouraged we are tempted to give up. Prayer here probably means more than repeating certain words endlessly. It is more likely our total lives as our effort to serve God and bring God's kingdom to this earth. The state of the world is often enough to discourage good people. The story says, "Don't give up!"

The widow is an especially good model for those called to act to correct the injustices of this world in unconven-tional or annoying ways. They, too, should hear the mes-sage: no matter how powerless you feel, don't give up!

Then Jesus told them a parable about their need to pray always and not to lose heart. He said, "In a certain city there was a judge who neither feared God nor had respect for people. In that city there was a widow who kept coming to him and saying, 'Grant me justice against my opponent.' For a while he refused; but later he said to himself, 'Though I have no fear of God and no respect for anyone, yet because this widow keeps bothering me, I will grant her justice, so that she may not wear me out by continually coming.'" And the Lord said, "Listen to what the unjust judge says. And will not God grant justice to his chosen ones who cry to him day and night? Will he delay long in helping them? I tell you, he will quickly grant justice to them."

Luke 18:1-8a

Entry into Jerusalem

Since Chapter 9 of Luke, Jesus has been leading his disciples, and us, on the journey to Jerusalem. Now he comes to the Mount of Olives, just east of Jerusalem. Here Jesus is planning a demonstration. He sends two disciples with detailed instructions to prepare by bringing him a colt. Jesus was a poor man who made his long journeys on foot. But for this final mile on which he wanted to demonstrate his royalty, he borrowed a colt to ride. This triumphal entry into Jerusalem is a moment of joy and peace which reminds us a little of Luke's description of Christmas. Throughout his public life Jesus had tried to avoid being called king. But now, on the eve of his death, he encourages the crowds who acclaim him as king. Perhaps it is only as we approach death that we can let people know who we really are.

After he had said this, he went on ahead, going up to Jerusalem.

When he had come near Bethphage and Bethany, at the

place called the Mount of Olives, he sent two of the disciples, saying, "Go into the village ahead of you, and as you enter it you will find tied there a colt that has never been ridden. Untie it and bring it here. If anyone asks you, 'Why are you untying it?' just say this, 'The Lord needs it.'" So those who were sent departed and found it as he had told them. As they were untying the colt, its owners asked them, "Why are you untying the colt?" They said, "The Lord needs it." Then they brought it to Jesus; and after throwing their cloaks on the colt, they set Jesus on it. As he rode along, people kept spreading their cloaks on the road. As he was now approaching the path down from the Mount of Olives, the whole multitude of the disciples began to praise God joyfully with a loud voice for all the deeds of power that they had seen, saying,

"Blessed is the king
who comes in the name of the Lord!
Peace in heaven,
and glory in the highest heaven!"

Some of the Pharisees in the crowd said to him, "Teacher, order your disciples to stop." He answered, "I tell you, if these were silent, the stones would shout out."

Luke 19:28-40

The triumphal procession passes over the Mount of Olives to a spot from which they have a clear view of Jerusalem. Today on the Mount of Olives you can visit a small church that commemorates this spot. As you look over the altar a large window presents a tremendous panorama of the city of Jerusalem, with the golden Muslim Dome of the Rock dominating the view on the spot where the great temple built by Herod dominated it in Jesus' time. The church is called *Dominus Flevit,* "The Lord Wept."

In sharp contrast to the joyful acclamations of the crowd, Jesus weeps when he sees the beautiful city they are approaching, knowing the utter devastation the Roman armies would wreck on it in A.D. 70. He utters a lament that comes from the bottom of his heart. He came to bring peace to this city he loved so much, but they could not recognize the gift. "Peace" in biblical language is more than the absence of war; it is the fullness of life God gives. All his life Jesus has been struggling to bring peace to these people. Only now does he seem to have given up hope for their conversion. Perhaps Luke puts this incident into his Gospel to give us comfort at the times when we lose hope of accomplishing the good things we set out to accomplish. The letting go of hope is painful for the dedicated servant of the Lord, as it was for Jesus.

> As he came near and saw the city, he wept over it, saying, "If you, even you, had only recognized on this day the things that make for peace! But now they are hidden from your eyes. Indeed, the days will come upon you, when your enemies will set up ramparts around you and surround you, and hem you in on every side. They will crush you to the ground, you and your children within you, and they will not leave within you one stone upon another; because you did not recognize the time of your visitation from God."

Luke 19:41-44

The Sadducees and the Resurrection

From the Mount of Olives Jesus continued his journey into Jerusalem and then to the temple, where he continued to teach. In Galilee, the main religious leaders with whom Jesus argued had been the Pharisees. In Jerusalem, the Sadducees come into the story for the first time in Luke's Gospel. They were the aristocratic class, mostly priests, so Jerusalem was their territory. Theologically, they were conservative. They accepted only the first five books of the Bible, the Torah, as authoritative. The Pharisees also believed in the rest of the Hebrew Scriptures and in oral tradition. This gave the Pharisees more flexibility, more ability to develop new doctrines. (It reminds one a bit of the difference between Protestants and Catholics today. Protestants generally base their faith on Scripture alone; Catholics on Scripture and tradition.) Two important things in which the Pharisees had come to believe were life after death and the existence of angels. In both these areas Jesus agreed with the Pharisees rather than the Sadducees.

Some Sadducees came to Jesus with a question which was not a question honestly seeking an answer at all but a clever attempt to show the absurdity of the Pharisees' belief in resurrection. The question is based on the levirate law, which required a man whose brother had died childless to marry the brother's widow in order to have children who would be legally considered the children of the deceased brother. The purpose of the law was to enable the deceased brother to live on through these fictional children. Some tribal cultures have laws of this kind even today. To make their point, the Sadducees imagine an absurd situation in which a woman had married seven brothers in a row. If there is a resurrection, whose husband will she then be? They are making fun of the Pharisees' belief in resurrection. This is religious gamesmanship. They have proposed a riddle to which they are sure there is no answer.

Jesus' answer shows how badly they have misunderstood the afterlife. It is a state quite different from the present one. In the resurrected life there is no death, and therefore no need for marriage and the bringing forth of children to keep the race alive. We will be like the angels, who do not die and do not marry. In Catholic tradition, those who practice celibacy are sometimes seen as anticipating the heavenly condition when there will be no more marriage or childbearing.

There is little clear description of heaven in Scripture. When we try too hard to imagine it we are likely to fall into pictures as absurd as that of the wife married to seven brothers. Probably the clearest statement on the subject is Paul's, "No eye has seen, no ear has heard, no mind has conceived what God has prepared for those who love him" (1 Corinthians 2:9 NIV).

Some Sadducees, those who say there is no resurrection, came to him and asked him a question, "Teacher, Moses wrote for us that if a man's brother dies, leaving a wife but no children, the man shall marry the widow and raise up children for his brother. Now there were seven brothers; the first married, and died childless; then the second and the third married her, and so in the same way all seven died childless. Finally the woman also died. In the resurrection, therefore, whose wife will the woman be? For the seven had married her."

Jesus said to them, "Those who belong to this age marry and are given in marriage; but those who are considered worthy of a place in that age and in the resurrection from the dead neither marry nor are given in marriage. Indeed they cannot die anymore, because they are like angels and are children of God, being children of the resurrection. And the fact that the dead are raised Moses himself showed, in the story about the bush, where he speaks of the Lord as the God of Abraham, the God of Isaac, and the God of Jacob. Now he is God not of the dead, but of the living; for to him all of them are alive." Then some of the scribes answered, "Teacher, you have spoken well." For they no longer dared to ask him another question.

Luke 20:27-40

—⁓—

Questions for Reflection

1. Who do you think are like the rich man and Lazarus in the world today?

2. After death Lazarus was "with Abraham." With whom would you like to be after death?

3. Do you agree with Jesus that wealth makes it difficult to enter the kingdom of heaven? Give examples to support your answer.

4. What example do you know of someone like the widow in Luke 18 who persevered in prayer or in seeking out justice for a long time before being answered?

5. Jesus wept over the destruction he saw coming to Jerusalem. What in the world today makes you feel like weeping?

6. Two of the passages in this chapter hint at how Jesus imagined heaven (Luke 16:23; Luke 20:34-36). How do you imagine heaven?

Suggestions for Further Reading

Luke 2:36-38; 4:25-26; I Kings 17:1-7;
Luke 7:11-17; 18:1-8; 21:1-4; 20:45-47:
Widows

CHAPTER TEN

More Widows and the Last Supper

Oppressors of Widows

THROUGHOUT CHAPTER 20 OF LUKE'S GOSPEL Jesus has been teaching the people in the temple. At the very end of the chapter he shifts his attention to the disciples. The people are still there in the background, but this particular teaching is aimed especially at the disciples. He tells them to beware of the scribes. He is not referring only to the learned canon lawyers of his day. He sees the potential scribe inside each disciple, and he is warning them as future leaders of the Church not to become scribes. Two things characterize the scribes: they take delight in the perks that come with their position of spiritual leadership, and, more seriously, they do not accept the responsibilities to the underprivileged that should go with their position. Instead of providing for poor widows as Scripture requires, they enrich themselves at the expense of these helpless women.

> In the hearing of all the people he said to the disciples, "Beware of the scribes, who like to walk around in long robes, and love to be greeted with respect in the market-places, and to have the best seats in the synagogues and places of honor at banquets. They devour widows' houses and for the sake of appearance say long prayers. They will receive the greater condemnation."

> *Luke 20:45-47*

A Generous Widow

In the next verses, Luke presents a real widow, one of these marginalized people whose houses the wealthy scribes devour. What a contrast she is to them! She makes a remarkable donation to the collection box in the temple. It is remarkable because of how small it is. The coins, "lepta," she contributes are the smallest that existed at that time, so comparable to our penny. But what is more remarkable is that what she gives is all she has to live on! The Greek says literally that she gave "all the life that she had." She reminds us of people today who have very little life, either because of extreme physical handicaps or because they are old and close to death, yet give all they have with generosity. Generosity is measured not by how much one gives, but by how much one holds back.

Perhaps as Jesus looked tenderly at this poor widow he was thinking of his widowed mother who in a few days would give all that she had on Calvary.

> He looked up and saw rich people putting their gifts into the treasury; he also saw a poor widow put in two small copper coins. He said, "Truly I tell you, this poor widow has put in more than all of them; for all of them have contributed out of their abundance, but she out of her poverty has put in all she had to live on."

Luke 21:1-4

The Chief Priests and Judas

In the next section the scene shifts to the chief priests and their scribes. In Galilee, Jesus' chief opponents had been the Pharisees, but in Jerusalem, power is held by the chief priests who serve in the temple there. Throughout the Passion, it is they rather than the Pharisees who will dominate. These religious leaders whom Jesus has criticized so sharply will have their revenge. It is hard for them to find a way to do this because the common people love Jesus. The priests do not want to risk a riot at Passover. An unexpected opportunity arises: one of Jesus' closest associates offers to find a way for them to arrest Jesus at a time when the people are not there to protect him.

It is hard to know what motivated Judas. He had been honored to be selected as one of the twelve closest followers of Jesus. He had listened to Jesus' teaching and witnessed his miracles. But as Jesus' life moved toward its climax he turned against his master. Perhaps he was tired of the life of poverty Jesus' followers led. Perhaps he sensed that, after all, Jesus was not going to be the kind of Messiah he had hoped for, and chose to jump ship while he could still profit by doing so.

> Now the festival of Unleavened Bread, which is called the Passover, was near. The chief priests and the scribes were looking for a way to put Jesus to death, for they were afraid of the people. Then Satan entered into Judas called Iscariot, who was one of the twelve; he went away and conferred with the chief priests and officers of the temple police about how he might betray him to them. They were greatly pleased and agreed to give him money. So he consented and began to look for an opportunity to betray him to them when no crowd was present.

Luke 22:1-6

Passover

Passover is the feast when Jews celebrate their identity as the people liberated from the slavery of Egypt by the power of God, and the time they hand the Exodus story on to their children. Perhaps Jesus chose this feast for his final meal with his disciples so that the memory of the Exodus could strengthen them for the ordeal ahead, as it has strengthened Jews through so many centuries.

At the time of Jesus, Passover was combined with the feast of Unleavened Bread, which celebrated the first harvest of the year. Bread in biblical times was leavened like our sour dough bread, with a fermented bit of old dough. However, to celebrate the new season all the old dough was discarded and fresh, unleavened bread was baked.

This double feast, Passover and Unleavened Bread, was a time of rejoicing in the Jews' special covenant relationship with God, and of hope that God would continue to care for them in the new season that was beginning. At the time of Jesus, the lambs to be eaten at Passover were first sacrificed in the temple. Thousands of pilgrims crowded the temple courtyards while the priests slaughtered their lambs according to the ritual of sacrifice. Then each father brought the meat home for the family meal. The law prescribed that the lamb be eaten in a family group, but Jesus chose to eat it with his disciples. Perhaps he wanted them to realize that they were the beginning of the Church, which was to become a new kind of family.

When the great feast of Passover arrived, Jesus sent his friends Peter and John to prepare the celebration. Jesus likes to send disciples off in pairs (Luke 10:1; 9:52; 19:29), as the early Christian missionaries went in pairs (Acts 8:14; 13:2; 15:36-40). To prepare the Passover meal was a serious responsibility, as it is in Jewish homes today. Peter and John probably felt the same mix of excitement and nervousness members of liturgy committees feel as they prepare for the Holy Week services. Jesus himself gave them detailed directions, like those he gave the disciples who prepared for the triumphal entry into Jerusalem. He is not merely a victim; he takes an active and willing part in the events that are coming. We see this by the way he takes control of the Passover plans.

> Then came the day of Unleavened Bread, on which the Passover lamb had to be sacrificed. So Jesus sent Peter and John, saying, "Go and prepare the Passover meal for us that we may eat it."
> They asked him, "Where do you want us to make preparations for it?" "Listen," he said to them, "when you have

entered the city, a man carrying a jar of water will meet you; follow him into the house he enters and say to the owner of the house, 'The teacher asks you, "Where is the guest room, where I may eat the Passover with my disciples?"' He will show you a large room upstairs, already furnished. Make preparations for us there." So they went and found everything as he had told them; and they prepared the Passover meal.

Luke 22:7-13

Jesus' first words set the tone for the meal. The Greek text says literally, "With desire have I desired to eat this meal with you." He begins by opening his heart to let us know how much this meal means to him. It is much like the desire he has to share the Eucharistic meal with us.

In the same sentence he makes clear the special meaning of this meal. It is the meal "before I suffer." The cross overshadows this festive table.

The Passover ritual called for four cups of wine. Jesus gives thanks for the first cup according to custom and shares it among the apostles. He then blesses a loaf of bread and breaks it. Here he adds something altogether new to the Passover ritual. He says, "This is my body, which is given for you." The broken bread becomes his body, soon to be broken for us. The group would have continued the Passover ritual, eating the lamb and bitter herbs, asking the ritual questions that lead into the retelling of the Exodus story, singing psalms. Luke passes over all this until the final cup of wine where Jesus again adds something altogether new: "This cup that is poured out for you is the new covenant in my blood." The cup poured out, like the bread broken, connects the Eucharist with the death of Jesus, when he willingly poured out his life for us.

Blood in Scripture is a symbol of life. At Mount Sinai, when God wanted to establish a covenant relationship with Israel, a lamb was killed and its blood, representing life, was sprinkled on God's altar and on the people (Exodus 34:3-8). The ritual proclaimed that they were entering into covenant, that God and the people of Israel would henceforth share the same life. Remembering that scene, Jesus says that a new covenant is being established, not in the blood of an animal this time, but in his own blood.

> When the hour came, he took his place at the table, and the apostles with him. He said to them, "I have eagerly desired to eat this Passover with you before I suffer; for I tell you, I will not eat it until it is fulfilled in the kingdom of God." Then he took a cup, and after giving thanks he said, "Take this and divide it among yourselves; for I tell you that from now on I will not drink of the fruit of the vine until the kingdom of God comes." Then he took a loaf of bread, and when he had given thanks, he broke it and gave it to them, saying, "This is my body, which is given for you. Do this in remembrance of me." And he did the same with the cup after supper, saying, "This cup that is poured out for you is the new covenant in my blood."

Luke 22:14-20

Judas, one of the twelve Jesus chose so carefully after a night of prayer, shares in the Eucharist. He is a warning that receiving sacraments does not guarantee salvation. When Jesus announces that one of those at table with him will betray him, they wonder who he means.

But they all betray him in a more subtle way. Contrary to all that he has taught them, they begin to argue about which of them will be the greatest. Once more, in the setting of this sacred meal, Jesus explains to the apostles that they are not to lord it over others, but to serve them, as Jesus serves us, even giving his life for us. It is such a radically new concept of authority that after two thousand years we still find it difficult to grasp.

Despite the rebuke, Jesus values the apostles, and he promises them positions of honor in his kingdom. He is grateful even for the very imperfect support they have given him.

> "...But see, the one who betrays me is with me, and his hand is on the table. For the Son of Man is going as it has been determined, but woe to that one by whom he is betrayed!" Then they began to ask one another, which one of them it could be who would do this.
>
> A dispute also arose among them as to which one of them was to be regarded as the greatest. But he said to them, "The kings of the Gentiles lord it over them; and those in authority over them are called benefactors. But not so with you; rather the greatest among you must become like the youngest, and the leader like one who serves. For who is greater, the one who is at the table or the one who serves? Is it not the one at the table? But I am among you as one who serves.
>
> "You are those who have stood by me in my trials; and I confer on you, just as my Father has conferred on me, a kingdom, so that you may eat and drink at my table in my kingdom, and you will sit on thrones judging the twelve tribes of Israel.

Luke 22:21-30

Now Jesus turns to Peter, but he does not call him by the name he gave him, "Rock." Peter will not be much of a rock in the coming events, so Jesus reverts to his old name, Simon. He tells him that all the disciples are entering into a time of severe trial, but Jesus has prayed especially for him. (The "you" in the first part of the sentence is plural; in the second part of the sentence it is singular.) Jesus knows that Peter will deny him, but he does not even mention that, as if it is not important. Instead, he jumps to what Peter will do after his conversion, after he "turns back." Then, as a repentant sinner, he will strengthen others. The one of the eleven whose sin is most conspicuous will also, after his repentance, be the one to lead and strengthen the others.

> "Simon, Simon, listen! Satan has demanded to sift all of you like wheat, but I have prayed for you that your own faith may not fail; and you, when once you have turned back, strengthen your brothers." And he said to him, "Lord, I am ready to go with you to prison and to death!" Jesus said, "I tell you, Peter, the cock will not crow this day, until you have denied three times that you know me."

> *Luke 22:31-34*

Jesus continues to try to help the apostles to understand the time of trial into which they are entering that night. He reminds them, a bit wistfully, of the bright days of their mission in Galilee, when he sent them out without a purse, bag or extra pair of sandals. They were to depend on the hospitality of those to whom they brought good news. They were never disappointed. But now things have changed and they have to expect struggle and conflict, not friendly hospitality. They need resources to deal with the present situation. Figuratively, he says they need a sword for the battle to come. As we do so often, they take him literally without grasping the real message. When they produce two swords, he dismisses the subject abruptly: "It is enough!" On the Mount of Olives they would draw the swords. Jesus would tell them to stop, and he would heal the man they wounded (22:49-51). Jesus calls his followers to struggle, but not to violence.

He said to them, "When I sent you out without a purse, bag, or sandals, did you lack anything?" They said, "No, not a thing." He said to them, "But now, the one who has a purse must take it, and likewise a bag. And the one who has no sword must sell his cloak and buy one. For I tell you, this Scripture must be fulfilled in me, 'And he was counted among the lawless'; and indeed what is written about me is being fulfilled." They said, "Lord, look, here are two swords." He replied, "It is enough."

Luke 22:35–38

This ends Luke's version of Jesus' farewell address. Jesus prepared the apostles for the ordeal of the Passion by nurturing them with both the Eucharist and his final words, which recapitulated much of what he had been teaching them throughout. Many Old Testament leaders had done the same. These farewell addresses usually look back over what the dying man has already shared with his disciples and forward to how they are to carry on his work after his death.

Those who reflect on the dying process today emphasize the importance of this final sharing of a parent or spouse with family members. They call us to facilitate it if we can and to honor legacies that have been handed on to us by our loved ones toward the end of their lives.

Questions for Reflection

1. What example of generosity have you seen that is like that of the widow who gave all that she had?

2. When have you been like Peter and John, preparing a special celebration for your family or other group? How did the responsibility make you feel?

3. What do you know from friends or reading about how Jews celebrate Passover today?

4. Why do you think Jesus chose the Passover meal as the last he shared with his disciples before his death?

5. How does reading Luke's account of the Last Supper help you to appreciate the Eucharist?

6. Why do you think Jesus chose Peter as a leader in his church? What kind of people are chosen as leaders in the Church today?

7. Is there a parent or other person whose last words have been important to you? What last words would you like to say to those you leave behind?

Suggestion for Further Reading
John 13–17 (John's version of Jesus' last discourse)

CHAPTER ELEVEN

The Passion

Prayer on the Mount of Olives

Luke's description of Jesus' agony is quite different from that of the other evangelists. It begins and ends with an exhortation to all of the disciples (including us) to pray at times of crisis. In Matthew and Mark this exhortation is more specifically to the chief apostles, Peter, James and John. The others are only told to rest while Jesus prays. The whole point of the story, as Luke tells it, is that Jesus, who spent time in prayer before every major event of his life, including his death, is a model of prayer for all of us.

In this scene as in no other we are allowed to witness the inner experience of Jesus. Luke, and only Luke, describes it as an "agony." The Greek word which is used here does not have quite the connotation that "agony" usually has for us. It refers to the extreme efforts of a wrestler or other athlete, or a warrior. Jesus is tensing his whole being in his mighty struggle with Satan. The inner struggle is so extreme that sweat pours from him as freely as blood pours from a wound. (Luke does not say that he actually sweat blood.) It is a struggle we all know well: the struggle to accept what God wills for us when it goes against all our instincts.

Even at this time of extreme trial, Jesus calls God "Father"—not a title commonly used in the Hebrew Scriptures. Luke wants us to know that throughout the Passion Jesus never loses the awareness of his special relationship with the Father. For that reason, he shows Jesus calling on his Father here at the beginning of the Passion and again at the end, when he will pray, "Father, into thy hands I commend my spirit."

He came out and went, as was his custom, to the Mount of Olives; and the disciples followed him. When he reached the place, he said to them, "Pray that you may not come into the time of trial." Then he withdrew from them about a stone's throw, knelt down, and prayed, "Father, if you are willing, remove this cup from me; yet, not my will but yours be done." Then an angel from heaven appeared to him and gave him strength. In his anguish he prayed more earnestly, and his sweat became like great drops of blood falling down on the ground. When he got up from prayer, he came to the disciples and found them sleeping because of grief, and he said to them, "Why are you sleeping? Get up and pray that you may not come into the time of trial."

Luke 22:39-46

Non-Violent Resistance

While Jesus is gently chiding the disciples, an armed crowd arrives, led by Judas. In a panic, the disciples produce the swords they had mentioned at the Last Supper. Jesus had dismissed the idea of swords then, but now that the crisis has arrived they ask if they should use them. However, like us sometimes, they do not wait for an answer. The situation was clearly urgent, and violence seemed the obvious response. One of the disciples cut off the ear of one of the attackers. Only after the fact could Jesus make himself heard. He forbade further violence, a message Luke wanted his readers of all ages to take as directed to themselves.

Luke adds a moving incident not mentioned in any other Gospel. Jesus touched the man who had been injured and healed him. Even in the midst of this chaotic scene, Jesus is a healer and a teacher. His example illustrates his often-repeated teaching about loving our enemies. His calm, dignified response to those attacking him is a model of non-violent resistance to evil.

While he was still speaking, suddenly a crowd came,
and the one called Judas, one of the twelve, was leading
them. He approached Jesus to kiss him; but Jesus said to
him, "Judas, is it with a kiss that you are betraying the Son
of Man?" When those who were around him saw what was
coming, they asked, "Lord, should we strike with the
sword?" Then one of them struck the slave of the high
priest and cut off his right ear. But Jesus said, "No more of
this!" And he touched his ear and healed him. Then Jesus
said to the chief priests, the officers of the temple police,
and the elders who had come for him, "Have you come out
with swords and clubs as if I were a bandit? When I was
with you day after day in the temple, you did not lay hands
on me. But this is your hour, and the power of darkness!"

Luke 22:47-53

Peter Follows and Stumbles

The rest of the disciples disappear from the story at this
point, but Peter follows Jesus and stays throughout the night
in spite of the embarrassment he suffers when others recognize him as one of the prisoner's followers. But having greater
courage than the others also leads him to greater sin. Three
times he denies his Lord. This is amazing when we remember
that at the Last Supper Jesus had promised to pray very especially for Peter. It seems that even Jesus' prayers are not
always answered!

The story of Peter's denial is told by all the Gospel writers, but only Luke adds the touching detail, "The Lord
turned and looked at Peter." Jesus has not given up on
Peter; through his eyes he reaches out to reconnect with
him, to bring back the memory of the meal they had shared
a few hours before. There is a church in Jerusalem today
that commemorates this moment. It is called "St. Peter at
the Cockcrow." The surprising thing is that this memorial

to Peter's sin is a beautiful church, full of light and of green, the color of hope. On the walls are painted Peter and other great penitents such as the Prodigal Son and Mary Magdalene. Peter, with a remarkable stretch of the imagination, is painted in elaborate robes with the papal triple crown on his head. Beneath him are the words from Luke's Gospel, "Once you have turned back, strengthen your brothers" (Luke 22:31). It is a church that celebrates repentance, and the great holiness that is possible for the repentant sinner.

Then they seized him and led him away, bringing him into the high priest's house. But Peter was following at a distance. When they had kindled a fire in the middle of the courtyard and sat down together, Peter sat among them. Then a servant-girl, seeing him in the firelight, stared at him and said, "This man also was with him." But he denied it, saying, "Woman, I do not know him." A little later someone else, on seeing him, said, "You also are one of them." But Peter said, "Man, I am not!" Then about an hour later still another kept insisting, "Surely this man also was with him; for he is a Galilean." But Peter said, "Man, I do not know what you are talking about!" At that moment, while he was still speaking, the cock crowed. The Lord turned and looked at Peter. Then Peter remembered the word of the Lord, how he had said to him, "Before the cock crows today you will deny me three times." And he went out and wept bitterly.

Luke 22:54–62

Encounters on the Way of the Cross

Jesus was condemned to death and led to Calvary. The Roman soldiers were permitted to press natives into service for such jobs as carrying the crossbeam on which the crucifixion would take place. (The upright was permanently fixed at the place of crucifixion.) They found a man from Cyrene in North Africa for the job. We are not told anything about him except his name and place of origin, but he is given us as a model of what Jesus had called all disciples to do, take up their cross and follow him (Luke 9:23, 14:27). He must have been a kind of special patron for the other African Christians from Cyrene who were leaders in the early Church (Acts 11:20; 13:1).

Only Luke tells us about the women from Jerusalem who also follow Jesus on the Way of the Cross. They lament his suffering. Jesus turns to them kindly, but sadly, and gives them, and us, another glimpse into his inner experience. We already know that as he entered into Jerusalem he wept over the destruction that would come to it in A.D. 70. Now we see that he experiences his own passion against the backdrop of that great disaster. So he tells the women that there is less reason to weep over him than over themselves and their children. His words portray vividly the horror of what will happen to Jerusalem when the Romans lay siege to the city and eventually level it to the ground. For women of Jesus' time, the worst conceivable curse was to be unable to have children. Yet Jesus says that what will happen to Jerusalem will be so awful that it will reverse their whole value system. They will wish to be barren instead of seeing the terrible suffering of their children.

As they led him away, they seized a man, Simon of Cyrene, who was coming from the country, and they laid the cross on him, and made him carry it behind Jesus. A great number of the people followed him, and among them were women who were beating their breasts and wailing for him. But Jesus turned to them and said, "Daughters of Jerusalem, do not weep for me, but weep for yourselves and for your children. For the days are surely coming when they will say, 'Blessed are the barren, and the wombs that never bore, and the breasts that never nursed.' Then they will begin to say to the mountains, 'Fall on us';

and to the hills, 'Cover us.' For if they do this when the wood is green, what will happen when it is dry?"

Luke 23:26-31

Companions on the Way

Throughout his life, Jesus had chosen the company of the outcasts, tax collectors, prostitutes and sinners. It seems fitting that he was to die surrounded by prisoners condemned to death.

Two others also, who were criminals, were led away to be put to death with him. When they came to the place that is called The Skull, they crucified Jesus there with the criminals, one on his right and one on his left.

Luke 23:32, 33

A Model of Forgiveness

Luke alone among the Gospels gives us Jesus' words from the cross, "Father, forgive them; for they do not know what they are doing." Again, Luke wants us to see Jesus as an outstanding model of the forgiveness of enemies which he has always preached. This is especially a model for the dying. It is their last opportunity to choose forgiveness for hurts that may have rankled for a lifetime.

Next, Luke shows us the varied reactions of those present to Jesus' suffering. Luke, who is not a Jew, always tries to show the ordinary Jewish people in the best possible light. Here he describes them simply as "watching." They have always been Jesus' supporters. They do not have the courage or conviction to fight their religious authorities. But neither do they really support them. They are in an in-between state which may well lead to conversion. Their leaders, on the other hand, mock Jesus, feeling triumph at what they think is his defeat. The soldiers carrying out the execution also make fun of their prisoner.

> When they came to the place that is called The Skull, they crucified Jesus there with the criminals, one on his right and one on his left. Then Jesus said, "Father, forgive them; for they do not know what they are doing." And they cast lots to divide his clothing. And the people stood by, watching; but the leaders scoffed at him, saying, "He saved others; let him save himself if he is the Messiah of God, his chosen one!" The soldiers also mocked him, coming up and offering him sour wine, and saying, "If you are the King of the Jews, save yourself!" There was also an inscription over him, "This is the King of the Jews."

Luke 23:33-38

Between Two Thieves

The two criminals who accompanied Jesus now hang one on his right side and one on his left. For Luke, Jesus is always the center of the picture. Jesus continues to be associated with the outcast to the end. But not all outcasts accept the salvation he offers them. One joins the mocking leaders. The other experiences an extraordinary conversion. Though he is suffering the torments of crucifixion, he acknowledges that he is receiving what he deserved, something few sufferers can do. Then, amazingly, he turns with hope to the man dying next to him, asking him to remember him when he comes into his kingdom! Jesus corrects him gently, "*Today* you will be with me in Paradise." With Jesus' death, salvation has already begun to break into the world. And this outsider, a criminal who was not one of Jesus' disciples before this moment, will get there before any of the disciples! Christian tradition has given him the name Saint Dismas, and he makes a good patron for those involved in pastoral work with inmates of death row. It is never too late for salvation.

> One of the criminals who were hanged there kept deriding him and saying, "Are you not the Messiah? Save yourself and us!" But the other rebuked him saying, "Do you not fear God, since you are under the same sentence of condemnation? And we indeed have been condemned justly, for we are getting what we deserve for our deeds, but this man has done nothing wrong." Then he said, "Jesus, remember me when you come into your kingdom." He replied, "Truly I tell you, today you will be with me in Paradise."

Luke 23:39-43

Varied Responses to Jesus' Death

For the third time in the Passion Narrative, Jesus addresses God as Father. At the beginning he begged his father that the cup would pass. On the cross he prayed to his Father to forgive his murderers. His final prayer is, "Father, into your hands I commend my spirit." It is a model for the death of a Christian.

Luke tells us of three reactions on the part of those present at Jesus' death. The most striking is that of the centurion, the Roman officer in charge of the execution. He is completely an "outsider." He does not even belong to Jesus' people. He is an official of the Roman oppressors who occupied Judea. As far as we know, he has never heard Jesus teach or witnessed one of his miracles. Yet he is deeply moved by this death, and proclaims with awe that this was indeed an innocent man he has executed. He represents all the "outsiders," the Gentiles, who will soon become followers of Jesus.

The Jewish crowds, the common people who had always loved Jesus and had watched his death with bated breath, now returned home beating their breasts. Jesus' death has led them to conversion. They will be among the crowds who join the infant church in Luke's second volume, the Acts of the Apostles.

For the first time, we learn that many of Jesus' friends had been watching the crucifixion from a distance. Most important among them are the women who had followed him from Galilee.

> It was now about noon, and darkness came over the whole land until three in the afternoon, while the sun's light failed; and the curtain of the temple was torn in two. Then Jesus, crying with a loud voice, said, "Father, into your hands I commend my spirit." Having said this, he breathed his last. When the centurion saw what had taken place, he praised God and said, "Certainly this man was innocent." And when all the crowds who had gathered there for this spectacle saw what had taken place, they returned home, beating their breasts. But all his acquaintances, including the women who had followed him from Galilee, stood at a distance, watching these things.

> *Luke 23:44-49*

The Women as Witnesses

Luke does not condemn whole groups, even the council that had condemned Jesus to death. He introduces a member of that council who, like Elizabeth and Zechariah and Simeon and Anna in the Infancy Narrative, was eagerly awaiting the kingdom of God. We are not told that he was a disciple of Jesus, but he provided the decent burial the male disciples were not there to provide.

The women disciples stayed and watched the burial. They would be the ones who were sure where the body of Jesus had been laid; so on Easter morning they would be the best witnesses that the body had disappeared. They returned home to prepare what was needed to show respect for the corpse, as women have done through the ages. But Luke, and only Luke, stresses that they then rested for the Sabbath in observance of Jewish law. From the Infancy Narrative on, Luke is always careful to show Jesus and his family as faithful observers of the law. That observance has gifted us all with Holy Saturday, the sacred pause between the Passion and the Resurrection. Human nature needs that pause. Perhaps even Jesus needed a full day in the tomb before beginning his risen life. Our culture which wants everything instantly is in violation not only of the Jewish law, but of the basic rhythm of human life.

> Now there was a good and righteous man named Joseph, who, though a member of the council, had not agreed to their plan and action. He came from the Jewish town of Arimathea, and he was waiting expectantly for the kingdom of God. This man went to Pilate and asked for the body of Jesus. Then he took it down, wrapped it in a linen cloth, and laid it in a rock-hewn tomb where no one had ever been laid. It was the day of Preparation, and the sabbath was beginning. The women who had come with him from Galilee followed, and they saw the tomb and how his body was laid. Then they returned, and prepared spices and ointments.
>
> On the sabbath they rested according to the commandment.

Luke 23:50–56

—⁓—

Questions for Reflection

1. When in your life have you had to pray like Jesus, "Father, if you are willing, remove this cup from me; yet not my will but yours be done"?

2. Whom do you know who, like Jesus when he healed the slave of the high priest, thought of others' needs even in time of great personal suffering?

3. Do you think violence is ever justifiable for a Christian? If so, when?

4. What large events of our times weigh on you as the coming destruction of Jerusalem weighed on Jesus?

5. What in Jesus' death as described by Luke is like the way you would want to die?

6. Joseph of Arimathea and the women worked hard to provide an honorable burial for Jesus. Whom do you know who does the same in our time?

7. With which character or characters in the story can you identify most easily: Simon of Cyrene, the women of Jerusalem, the Good Thief, the Centurion, Joseph of Arimathea, the women disciples? Why?

Suggestion for Further Reading

Mark 14:32-15:47 (Mark's account of the Passion)

CHAPTER TWELVE

The Empty Tomb

The Women

THE GOSPEL ACCOUNT OF THE RESURRECTION begins where the crucifixion ended, with the women. Throughout his Gospel, Luke
puts special emphasis on the role of women. In the passion
account, they provide continuity. They are the only witnesses
of the whole story: Jesus' preaching and miracles in Galilee, his
suffering and death, his burial and the empty tomb.

Presumably, the women had heard Jesus' predictions of
his death and resurrection, but they had forgotten them.
After staying with Jesus through his passion and death and
burial, they had rested on the Sabbath according to the law.
They must have been exhausted. But early the next morning, Sunday, they set out to anoint the body of Jesus. The
care-giving work of women has traditionally started at birth
and continued through the rituals connected with burial.
They were doing no more than women throughout the
ages had done. They did not yet believe in the
Resurrection. They were expecting to find a corpse in the
cave where they had seen it placed.

Even when they found the tomb empty, it did not occur
to them that Jesus had risen. They were simply perplexed.
When they saw two angels in dazzling clothes they were so
terrified they fell flat on their faces.

The angels helped them remember, at last, Jesus' words.
These women are so much like us. We are good people,
going about our duties faithfully, and we have heard the
words of Jesus. But we forget them. When things do not
turn out the way we expected, we are perplexed. We often
need an angel, a messenger, to remind us of what we know
but have forgotten. Sometimes we are called to be this

angel for someone else, calling the forgotten words of Jesus to mind.

Today, at the Church of the Holy Sepulcher in Jerusalem, lines of pilgrims wait their turn to do what the women did—walk into the tomb. It is not enough to stand outside and look at the tomb; one must enter into the experience of death with one's whole being. And, of course, they find it empty. When I had that experience, I was struck forcefully by the words of the angels, "Why do you look for the living among the dead? He is not here."

It can happen in our lives also that we go to a place or a kind of prayer where we once found Jesus, expecting to find him there again. But he is no longer there for us; he has moved on and we have to leave the empty tomb and follow him. The message is that Jesus is alive and therefore unpredictable.

The women brought the angels' message back to the apostles, but were not taken seriously, as women so often are not. Peter did go to see the empty tomb, but the angels did not appear to him. The women were the "angels" sent to him and he could not accept the message from them. It can happen to us, too, that on Easter we can see only the empty tomb because we have not listened to the messengers sent to us.

But on the first day of the week, at early dawn, the women who had come with him from Galilee came to the tomb, taking the spices that they had prepared. They found the stone rolled away from the tomb, but when they went in, they did not find the body. While they were perplexed about this, suddenly two men in dazzling clothes stood beside them. The women were terrified and bowed their faces to the ground, but the men said to them, "Why do you look for the living among the dead? He is not here, but has risen. Remember how he told you, while he was still in Galilee, that the Son of Man must be handed over to sinners, and be crucified, and on the third day rise again." Then they remembered his words, and returning from the tomb, they told all this to the eleven and to all the rest. Now it was Mary Magdalene, Joanna, Mary the mother of James, and the other women with them who told this to the apostles. But these words seemed to them an idle tale, and they did not believe them. But Peter got up and ran to the tomb; stooping and looking in, he saw the linen cloths by themselves; then he went home, amazed at what had happened.

Luke 24:1-12

Emmaus

Next Luke tells us about two disciples, Cleopas and a companion, probably his wife, since they seem to live in the same house. They are on a journey. (Luke likes things to happen during journeys.) This is a journey of seven miles away from Jerusalem. Jesus was always journeying toward Jerusalem; that this journey is in the opposite direction already makes us suspicious that all is not well.

Jesus meets them as they walk along and asks them what they are discussing. They thought they knew Jesus very well, yet they did not recognize him. Every human being is a mystery, and sometimes we do not recognize those we think we know well.

Not recognizing this mysterious stranger, they tell him the story, including the poignant words, "We *had* hoped that he was the one to redeem Israel." These disciples loved Jesus, but they had lost hope. It can happen in our lives also that when things do not turn out as we expected we lose hope and fail to recognize Jesus who in reality is walking the road with us.

Jesus listens patiently, lets them pour out their tale, before he speaks. It is a good example for us when we meet troubled people. Only after careful listening does he give them a little Bible teaching. They knew the Scriptures well, or thought they did. But they never connected what they read in Scripture with the experience of Jesus' passion and death they had just gone through. The biblical message is not always clear from the book itself; it needs to be interpreted by the Jesus who walks with us through life. In this story we see that the experiences of our lives may not make sense to us until they are illuminated by the word of Scripture, and much in Scripture can have no meaning for us until we have the life experience that explains it. This little drama says much about the place of the study of Scripture in Christian life.

Now on that same day two of them were going to a village called Emmaus, about seven miles from Jerusalem, and talking with each other about all these things that had happened. While they were talking and discussing, Jesus himself came near and went with them, but their eyes were kept from recognizing him. And he said to them, "What are you discussing with each other while you walk along?" They stood still, looking sad. Then one of them, whose name was Cleopas, answered him, "Are you the only stranger in Jerusalem who does not know the things that have taken place there in these days?" He asked them, "What things?" They replied, "The things about Jesus of Nazareth, who was a prophet mighty in deed and word before God and all the people, and how our chief priests and leaders handed him over to be condemned to death and crucified him. But we had hoped that he was the one to redeem Israel. Yes, and besides all this, it is now the third day since these things took place. Moreover, some women of our group astounded us. They were at the tomb early this morning, and when they did not find his body there, they came back and told us that they had indeed seen a vision of angels who said that he was alive. Some of those who were with us went to the tomb and found it just as the women had said; but they did not see him." Then he said to them, "Oh, how foolish you are, and how slow of heart to believe all that the prophets have declared! Was it not necessary that the Messiah should suffer these things and then enter into his glory?" Then beginning with Moses and all the prophets, he interpreted to them the things about himself in all the Scriptures.

Luke 24:13-27

———

The two disciples did not know who it was who was giving them this instruction on Scripture. But they felt something special in his presence. Later, they would remember that their hearts were burning within them as they walked with him. They urged him to spend the night in their home. They did not know who he was, but they wanted to maintain the relationship they were beginning to feel with him. This decision to welcome a stranger into their home was perhaps the most important thing they ever did. This is a good story to remember when we are questioning whether we should take some stranger into our lives.

He agreed to accept their hospitality. At their meal, he blessed and broke the bread, as he had done so many times with them. Only then were their eyes opened. Their experience is much like ours at Eucharist, in which we meet Jesus first in the Scripture, then in the breaking of the bread. Luke puts a great deal of emphasis on the meals Jesus shared with his disciples, both before the Resurrection and afterwards. They make him think of his community's experience of the Eucharist.

As they came near the village to which they were going, he walked ahead as if he were going on. But they urged him strongly, saying, "Stay with us, because it is almost evening and the day is now nearly over." So he went in to stay with them. When he was at the table with them, he took bread, blessed and broke it, and gave it to them. Then their eyes were opened, and they recognized him; and he vanished from their sight. They said to each other, "Were not our hearts burning within us while he was talking to us on the road, while he was opening the Scriptures to us?"

Luke 24:28-32

—∿∿—

It was late, and the two disciples had already walked seven miles, but they could not wait until morning. They hurried back to share the news of their experience of Jesus. Now they were traveling as they had with Jesus, toward Jerusalem. The journey to Emmaus was a process of coming to faith. The return journey was one of sharing faith. When they arrived, they found the disciples gathered, full of other news. The Lord had appeared to Simon Peter! They had discounted the word of the women, but the cumulative effect of these experiences was leading them to faith. This faith is built up first by sharing within the community; later they would be able to proclaim it to others also.

> That same hour they got up and returned to Jerusalem; and they found the eleven and their companions gathered together. They were saying, "The Lord has risen indeed, and he has appeared to Simon!" Then they told what had happened on the road, and how he had been made known to them in the breaking of the bread.

Luke 24:33-35

—∿∿—

Jerusalem

Suddenly Jesus himself appears in the midst of the disciples and greets them. They find it hard to believe even their own eyes; they think he is a mere ghost. In general, Jews put little value on disembodied souls; they would not feel that Jesus was really present unless he had a body. So he goes to great trouble to show them that he does. The tomb was empty for a reason. The disciples are a bit like us when Jesus is present in our lives but we find it hard to believe that it is really him. It was all too much for the disciples. Their feelings were confused. They rejoiced, yet they did not fully believe. We, too, can have mixed and confusing feelings at times about our relationship with Jesus.

> While they were talking about this, Jesus himself stood among them and said to them, Peace be with you." They were startled and terrified and thought that they were seeing a ghost. He said to them, "Why are you frightened and why do doubts arise in your hearts? Look at my hands and my feet; see that it is I myself. Touch me and see, for a ghost does not have flesh and bones as you see that I have." And when he had said this, he showed them his hands and his feet. While in their joy they were disbelieving and still wondering, he said to them, "Have you anything here to eat?" They gave him a piece of broiled fish, and he took it and ate in their presence.

> *Luke 24:36-43*

The risen Jesus is a great model for Scripture teachers. As he had on the way to Emmaus, he opens the minds of the disciples to the deeper meaning of the Scriptures they had always known. He uses Scripture to help them to understand both what had happened in his death and resurrection and what would happen as they became witnesses who could go out to proclaim the message to all nations. He emphasizes the continuity between the Old and New Testaments by specifying that their preaching should begin in the holy Jewish city of Jerusalem, but spread to the whole earth.

But these bewildered disciples are not yet ready to go out as apostles. (A disciple is one who learns from a master; an apostle is one sent out on a mission by the master.) They need to wait patiently where they are, in Jerusalem, until at Pentecost they are clothed with power from on high. These words give a feel for the dynamism of the mission into which the Spirit will propel them. There are times in our lives, too, when all we can do is remain in faithful observance of what we have been taught, waiting for the fresh movement of the Spirit to propel us onward.

Then he said to them, "These are my words that I spoke to you while I was still with you—that everything written about me in the law of Moses, the prophets, and the psalms must be fulfilled." Then he opened their minds to understand the Scriptures, and he said to them, "Thus it is written, that the Messiah is to suffer and to rise from the dead on the third day, and that repentance and forgiveness of sins is to be proclaimed in his name to all nations, beginning from Jerusalem. You are witnesses of these things. And see, I am sending upon you what my Father promised; so stay here in the city until you have been clothed with power from on high."

Luke 24:44-49

Ascension

Jesus and the disciples return to Bethany, where the triumphal entry into Jerusalem began. His final act is to bless the witnesses who will go out to the ends of the earth with his message. Now at last they understand who he is, and worship him. It can happen to us, too, that we do not understand a person until the moment he or she leaves us.

When he has left, they obey his instructions to return to Jerusalem to await the coming of the Spirit. There they continue to pray in the temple, as they always had. The temple symbolizes for Luke all the holiness of the Old Testament. He begins his Gospel with Zechariah receiving Gabriel's message in the temple and ends it with the infant Christian community praying in the temple. Luke's entire Gospel is enclosed by the Jerusalem Temple.

Then he led them out as far as Bethany, and, lifting up his hands, he blessed them. While he was blessing them, he withdrew from them and was carried up into heaven. And they worshiped him, and returned to Jerusalem with great joy; and they were continually in the temple blessing God.

Luke 24:50-53

In his second volume, the Acts of the Apostles, Luke will show how this frightened little community will be clothed with power from on high on Pentecost, and the Gospel will spread out from Jerusalem to the ends of the earth.

Questions for Reflection

1. When has a messenger from God helped you remember some word of Jesus you needed at a particular moment, as the angels helped the women remember Jesus' predictions of his death? Have you ever been called to be such a messenger?

2. When in your life have you been tempted to lose hope, as the two disciples on the road to Emmaus had?

3. Can you remember a person or book that suddenly showed you how the Scriptures applied to your life, as Jesus showed the two disciples?

4. When has welcoming a stranger into your home or into your life been a blessing for you, as it was for Cleopas and his companion?

5. When has something so exciting happened to you that you felt you could have walked seven miles at night to share it with friends?

6. When have you experienced a time of waiting for the coming of the Spirit?

Suggestion for Further Reading
John 20-21 (compare with Luke's
Resurrection story)

CHAPTER THIRTEEN

The Church Is Born

Introduction

THE ACTS OF THE APOSTLES IS A BOOK ABOUT the first great transition in the life of the Church. Its author, Luke, is writing a full generation after the events and probably sees what happened more clearly than anyone saw it while it was happening.

The story begins with a church centered in Peter in Jerusalem composed of Jews who observe the Jewish law. It is one among the many groups within Judaism, much as Benedictines, the Legion of Mary and Knights of Columbus are groups within Catholicism. The story ends with a church centered in Paul in Rome, containing a majority of Gentiles, generally not observing the Jewish law. This latter is the church known to Luke's readers and he wants to teach them to look back on the Jewish community from which the church was born with reverence and even a little nostalgia.

What he especially wants them to see is that this great transition from Jerusalem to Rome did not happen by chance. The Holy Spirit guided every stage, often in directions the human actors could never have anticipated. At turning points in the story God intervened by dreams, prophecies or visions.

There was both continuity and discontinuity in that time of transition. Luke emphasizes both the newness of the church created by the Holy Spirit and its continuity with its Jewish past. God wills both. God does not want the old Jewish-Christian church to die, but to expand into something much greater and very different. The process is not planned by any human being, but by God.

It is a lively story. The church goes through many

adventures in the process. The things that appear bad often turn out to be good. God is sometimes in the background but always in control.

This is not just a story about the first great transition in the life of the church. By studying this transition we learn a great deal about how the Spirit of God works in all the transitions of our lives.

The Ascension

Luke begins the Acts of the Apostles, as he ends his Gospel, with a description of the Ascension of Jesus. Jesus is taken up into a cloud. For biblical writers the cloud, mysterious source of life-giving rain, was a symbol of God's presence. This is clearly the ending of Jesus' being present on this earth in the ordinary human way. But before he leaves, Jesus promises a new kind of presence, the Holy Spirit. The disciples will be baptized, which means immersed, in this Spirit who will fill them with power that will enable them to spread the Gospel to the ends of the earth. Like Mary at the Annunciation, they are promised that the power of the Most High will come upon them. It is quite an amazing prophecy for this sad little band of disciples that has just lost its Master. In order to receive the Spirit, they must remain in Jerusalem, which for Luke represents Judaism, the old way of God's presence.

Jesus ordered the apostles not to leave Jerusalem, but to wait there for the promise of the Father.

> "This," he said, "is what you have heard from me; for John baptized with water, but you will be baptized with the Holy Spirit not many days from now."
> So when they had come together, they asked him, "Lord, is this the time when you will restore the kingdom to Israel?" He replied, "It is not for you to know the times or periods that the Father has set by his own authority. But you will receive power when the Holy Spirit has come upon you; and you will be my witnesses in Jerusalem, in all Judea and Samaria, and to the ends of the earth." When he

had said this, as they were watching, he was lifted up, and a cloud took him out of their sight.

Acts 1:4b-9

The Community in Waiting

After Jesus had ascended from the Mount of Olives the disciples returned to Jerusalem to wait for the gift of the Spirit. We imitate them in praying the novena in preparation for Pentecost each year. The difference was that they did not know how long they would have to wait. It must have been like the times in our lives when we are completely helpless and do not know what we should do. There is nothing to do but wait for God to take the initiative. These can be the most difficult times. The first Christians knew that it was important to remain together in one place with Mary and the relatives of Jesus praying and waiting. For Mary, these nine days must have brought back memories of the nine months she waited for the birth of Jesus. (Gregorian chant uses some of its Advent melodies also in the days before Pentecost.)

Then they returned to Jerusalem from the mount called Olivet, which is near Jerusalem, a sabbath day's journey away. When they had entered the city, they went to the room upstairs where they were staying, Peter, and John, and James, and Andrew, Philip and Thomas, Bartholomew and Matthew, James son of Alphaeus, and Simon the Zealot, and Judas son of James. All these were constantly devoting themselves to prayer, together with certain women, including Mary the mother of Jesus, as well as his brothers.

Acts 1:12-14

Pentecost

Like all other Jews, the community gathered in the room upstairs celebrated the feast of Pentecost. It was a day when Jews remembered the experience of Sinai, the mountain which was all on fire and filled with a mighty storm wind on the day when Moses climbed it to receive God's law. A Jewish commentary, or Targum, says that the Israelites at the foot of Sinai were united in one heart and constantly occupied in prayer during the week while they waited for God's manifestation. The little Christian community were much like their ancestors at Sinai.

While they were celebrating the old manifestation of God and the law that went with it, a new manifestation and law burst forth unexpectedly. Luke wants us to notice that these were not Jews who were tired of the old ways and ready to abandon them. It was when they were faithfully celebrating the old that the Spirit catapulted them into the new.

It was the morning of this Pentecost. It had been in the morning that Moses had climbed up Mount Sinai, and morning always suggests new beginnings. The disciples were all gathered together in the upper room when a violent wind, like that of Sinai, suddenly filled the whole house. Then fire came down from heaven, also reminiscent of Sinai. However, the fire took an unusual shape, that of tongues. The shape was a hint of the miracle that then took place: these simple Galileans began speaking in languages from all over the earth, languages of countries of which they had probably never heard.

It is significant that the tongues of fire rested on the heads of all the 120 disciples who were gathered. Not only the twelve apostles, but all of them were empowered to give witness to Jesus in languages they had never known before. This miraculous event points ahead to all of Christian history, in which even the most unlikely Christian is often empowered by the Spirit to speak the gospel in the words that can reach some particular person. The formal jargon of the catechism is a foreign language to most of those who need to be evangelized. Each of our hearts has its own language.

Yet the Spirit is not an individualistic gift. Each individual received it only because of being present in the one house where the event took place. It is the Spirit that builds community, breaking down the barriers of language which can separate us: not only nation from nation but even generation from generation. At Babel, the human race divided up because people could no longer understand each other. At Pentecost, the Spirit began a new process of understanding which can ultimately bring us all back together again.

One wonders what this experience was like for Mary. She had been overshadowed by the Spirit before in her life, at the time of the Annunciation. As a result, she had given birth to Jesus. Now the Spirit did not come on her alone but on the whole community. And this time the Spirit gave birth to the Church. She was a very old woman at this point, as age went at her time, but she was about to take on a whole new role as mother in the infant Church.

All this commotion—wind, fire, ordinary people speaking strange languages—gathered all the neighbors. Jerusalem was very densely populated, especially on the feast of Pentecost, when Jewish pilgrims from all over the world came there to pray. There were also a great many retired Jews from all over the world who had come to live their later years in the holy city, though they spoke the languages of the countries in which they had grown up and worked. I imagine them as a bit like the communities of retired Americans who live in Mexico. These pilgrims and retirees became the first group to be evangelized by the newborn Church. It can still be true that those who have taken time out from their ordinary busyness, or those able to retire from it, are in the best position to hear whatever new message God may send.

When the day of Pentecost had come, they were all together in one place. And suddenly from heaven there came a sound like the rush of a violent wind, and it filled the entire house where they were sitting. Divided tongues, as of fire, appeared among them, and a tongue rested on each of them. All of them were filled with the Holy Spirit and began to speak in other languages, as the Spirit gave them ability.

Now there were devout Jews from every nation under heaven living in Jerusalem. And at this sound the crowd gathered and was bewildered, because each one heard them speaking in the native language of each. Amazed and astonished, they asked, "Are not all these who are speaking Galileans? And how is it that we hear, each of us, in our own native language? Parthians, Medes, Elamites, and residents of Mesopotamia, Judea and Cappadocia, Pontus and Asia, Phrygia and Pamphylia, Egypt and the parts of Libya belonging to Cyrene, and visitors from Rome, both Jews and proselytes, Cretans and Arabs—in our own languages we hear them speaking about God's deeds of power."

Acts 2:1-11

The Spirit Speaks Through Peter

The reaction to the miracle of Pentecost, like the reaction to most of God's works, was divided. Everyone was amazed, but some were not comfortable with these strange goings on. They laughed and said the disciples must be drunk. It is easy to pass judgments that enable us to dismiss enthusiasts whose behavior does not conform to our standards.

Now we meet Peter, who will be the central human character for the first half of Acts. But Peter is never alone. He stands with the eleven other apostles around him, as the pope stands surrounded by the other bishops.

Peter addresses these Jews with a prophecy familiar to them from their Scripture. He wants them to understand that this startling new development is not a break with their sacred past, but a fulfillment of it. He reminds them that the prophet Joel promised a great pouring out of the Spirit. Perhaps Peter saw young people in the crowd as well as the retired population of Jerusalem, because he points out that when the Spirit comes both young and old will be transformed with new vision. The Spirit comes on all: men and women, rich and poor, old and young.

This is not a gentle sermon. Peter bluntly accuses the crowd of killing Jesus. If we do not recognize our sins we cannot grow. But the sermon is not a "downer." There is hope if they will repent and be baptized, that is, become part of the community of disciples.

All were amazed and perplexed, saying to one another, "What does this mean?" But others sneered and said, "They are filled with new wine."

But Peter, standing with the eleven, raised his voice and addressed them, "Men of Judea and all who live in Jerusalem, let this be known to you, and listen to what I say. Indeed, these are not drunk, as you suppose, for it is only nine o'clock in the morning. No, this is what was spoken through the prophet Joel:

'In the last days it will be, God declares,
that I will pour out my Spirit upon all flesh,
    and your sons and your daughters shall prophesy,
and your young men shall see visions,
    and your old men shall dream dreams.
Even upon my slaves, both men and women,
    in those days I will pour out my Spirit;
        and they shall prophesy. . . .' "

"You that are Israelites, listen to what I have to say: Jesus of Nazareth, a man attested to you by God with deeds of power, wonders, and signs that God did through him among you, as you yourselves know—this man, handed over to you according to the definite plan and foreknowledge of God, you crucified and killed by the hands of those outside the law. But God raised him up, having freed him

from death, because it was impossible for him to be held
in its power...."

Acts 2:12-24

—⁓—

Preachers know that a successful sermon is not one after
which people come gushing up to them telling them how
wonderful they are. After a successful sermon, people come
up to the preacher saying, "What should I do?" Peter's was a
successful sermon.

Now when they had heard this, they were cut to the
heart and said to Peter and to the other apostles, "Brothers,
what should we do?" Peter said to them, "Repent, and be
baptized every one of you in the name of Jesus Christ so
that your sins may be forgiven, and you may receive the
Holy Spirit ..."

Acts 2:37, 38

—⁓—

Questions for Reflection

1. The Ascension ended one kind of presence of Jesus
   among us and Pentecost began another. In human relationships does it ever happen that a person leaves yet
   becomes present in a different way?

2. Between the Ascension and Pentecost the disciples could
   only wait and pray. When has there been a time like that
   in your life?

3. It was while the disciples were celebrating the ancient
   feast of Pentecost that the Spirit came on them to lead
   them into a new era. Can you think of any new insight or
   direction that came out of an old celebration or religious
   practice?

4. Why do you think God used the symbols of wind and fire at Pentecost?

5. When have you experienced the problem of communication with those whose language is different from yours because of their age or background? Have you ever felt that the Holy Spirit helped to overcome this problem?

6. Can you think of religious people today who seem as strange to you as the disciples seemed to some in the Pentecost crowd?

7. Can you think of a time when, as Joel says, God's Spirit caused an old person to dream a significant dream?

Suggestions for Further Reading

Luke 1-2; Acts 1-2 (Luke parallels the infancy of Jesus and the infancy of the church.)

CHAPTER FOURTEEN

Miracles and Persecution

Healing of the Elderly Cripple

THE FIRST HEALING STORY IN ACTS GIVES US a vivid picture of the effects of Pentecost. The disciples continued to be fervent Jews, worshiping in the Jerusalem Temple as Jesus had. The Spirit helped them to remember things Jesus had taught them. He had sent them out two by two, never as lone rangers (Luke 10:11), so they continued to move about with companions.

Peter and John were going together to the Temple at three o'clock, the time of the afternoon service. At the gate of the temple they noticed a man who had been crippled from birth. He was over forty, a very old age in a time when life expectancy was much less than today. Every day his friends brought him to the temple gate to beg. This was not a man who was expecting any improvement in his life. After living so many years with his handicap, in advanced old age he only hoped for the handouts that would enable him to continue the life he was used to for a while longer.

He sees in Peter and John only one more possibility of a few coins. But Peter asks for his full attention. The crippled man looks at them. Peter admits that he has no money. Perhaps, like Jesus, he delegated someone else to handle the community's finances. Perhaps he realized, as charitable organizations today are realizing, that it is better to empower the poor to act themselves than to keep them dependent on our gifts. So he told the cripple, "In the name of Jesus Christ of Nazareth, rise and walk." But it is not enough to exhort the poor. Like Jesus, he bent down, stretched out his hand and raised the man. What a shock to an old man who had never moved independently in his life!

But this old man, unprepared as he was, rose to the occasion immediately. We might expect an elderly person taking his first steps to totter cautiously, but not so. He jumped up, and went into the temple with Peter and John, walking and leaping and praising God. Perhaps it is because he is such a vivid picture of the resurrected life given by the Spirit that his cure is the first miracle described after Pentecost. It is also the story read at daily Mass during Easter Week.

The Bible leaves us to imagine what the new life of this cripple would be like. It is no small challenge to start a whole new life at an advanced age.

One day Peter and John were going up to the temple at the hour of prayer, at three o'clock in the afternoon. And a man lame from birth was being carried in. People would lay him daily at the gate of the temple called the Beautiful Gate so that he could ask for alms from those entering the temple. When he saw Peter and John about to go into the temple, he asked them for alms. Peter looked intently at him, as did John, and said, "Look at us." And he fixed his attention on them, expecting to receive something from them. But Peter said, "I have no silver or gold, but what I have I give you; in the name of Jesus Christ of Nazareth, stand up and walk." And he took him by the right hand and raised him up; and immediately his feet and ankles were made strong. Jumping up, he stood and began to walk, and he entered the temple with them, walking and leaping and praising God. All the people saw him walking and praising God, and they recognized him as the one who used to sit and ask for alms at the Beautiful Gate of the temple; and they were filled with wonder and amazement at what had happened to him.

Acts 3:1-10

—⁓—

Everybody knew the crippled man who had sat begging at the gate of the temple for so many years. So a crowd gathered quickly. As at Pentecost, Peter used the opportunity of explaining the marvel that has aroused so much interest to preach the gospel. As at Pentecost, he did not hesitate to point an accusing finger at the audience: "You killed the author of life." But he went on, like Jesus on the cross, to acknowledge that they did not know what they were doing. And he called them to conversion. He knew that seeing the cripple given new life had opened the crowd to hearing the gospel. Today, too, it is seeing the power of Jesus in someone else's life that often opens a person to the gospel.

> While [the formerly crippled man] clung to Peter and John, all the people ran together to them in the portico called Solomon's Portico, utterly astonished. When Peter saw it, he addressed the people, "You Israelites, why do you wonder at this, or why do you stare at us, as though by our own power or piety we had made him walk? The God of Abraham, the God of Isaac, and the God of Jacob, the God of our ancestors has glorified his servant Jesus, whom you handed over and rejected in the presence of Pilate, though he had decided to release him. But you rejected the Holy and Righteous One and asked to have a murderer given to you, and you killed the Author of life, whom God raised from the dead. To this we are witnesses. And by faith in his name, his name itself has made this man strong, whom you see and know; and the faith that is through Jesus has given him this perfect health in the presence of all of you.
>
> "And now, friends, I know that you acted in ignorance, as did also your rulers. In this way God fulfilled what he had foretold through all the prophets, that his Messiah would suffer. Repent therefore, and turn to God so that your sins may be wiped out...."

Acts 3:11-19

The Good News Rejected

Like Jesus, the apostles were preaching in the temple. Like him, they were welcomed by the common people, but not by the "leaders," the religious authorities. In fact, it is fear of the people that restrained the authorities from expressing their hostility to Jesus and the apostles more violently (Luke 20:19; 22:2). One of the Old Testament passages most frequently quoted by the early Christians is from Psalm 118: "The stone the builders rejected has become the cornerstone." Jesus, though rejected by his own religious leaders, has become the cornerstone of the Church.

When Peter and John are brought to trial before the religious authorities we see the beginning of what will eventually be a total break between official Judaism and Christianity.

While Peter and John were speaking to the people, the priests, the captain of the temple, and the Sadducees came to them, much annoyed because they were teaching the people and proclaiming that in Jesus there is the resurrection of the dead. So they arrested them and put them in custody until the next day, for it was already evening. But many of those who heard the word believed; and they numbered about five thousand.

The next day their rulers, elders, and scribes assembled in Jerusalem, with Annas the high priest, Caiaphas, John, and Alexander, and all who were of the high-priestly family. When they had made the prisoners stand in their midst, they inquired, "By what power or by what name did you do this?" Then Peter, filled with the Holy Spirit, said to them, "Rulers of the people and elders, if we are questioned today because of a good deed done to someone who was sick and are asked how this man has been healed, let it be known to all of you, and to all the people of Israel, that this man is standing before you in good health by the name of Jesus Christ of Nazareth, whom you crucified, whom God raised from the dead. This Jesus is

'the stone that was rejected by you, the builders;

it has become the cornerstone.'
There is salvation in no one else, for there is no other name under heaven given among mortals by which we must be saved."

Acts 4:1-12

The authorities are amazed at the boldness of these poor, uneducated laymen. This boldness in witnessing to Jesus is a gift of the Spirit. When Peter and John speak so forcefully before the solemn court, everyone present must have felt that the world was turned upside down. Galilean peasants did not address the religious elite of Jerusalem in that way. They even insist, again, on blaming their hearers for the death of Jesus.

Such insubordination would ordinarily be quickly punished, but this situation was awkward for the authorities because of the presence of the man who had just been miraculously cured. It was hard to argue with him! In fact, the conclusion and climax of the story is the statement of his age. No one could imagine a marvel greater than the healing of a person of such advanced age.

People today often go on the same assumption: after a certain age there is no hope of improvement in a person. Jesus clearly does not accept the assumption. Father Bede Griffith, at eighty-two, said that he had experienced more growth in his last two years than in his whole previous life. Our surprise at this testimony is much like that of the Jews at the healing of the forty-year-old crippled man.

> Now when they saw the boldness of Peter and John and realized that they were uneducated and ordinary men, they were amazed and recognized them as companions of Jesus. When they saw the man who had been cured standing beside them, they had nothing to say in opposition. So they ordered them to leave the council while they discussed the matter with one another. They said, "What will

we do with them? For it is obvious to all who live in Jerusalem that a notable sign has been done through them; we cannot deny it. But to keep it from spreading further among the people, let us warn them to speak no more to anyone in this name." So they called them and ordered them not to speak or teach at all in the name of Jesus. But Peter and John answered them, "Whether it is right in God's sight to listen to you rather than to God, you must judge; for we cannot keep from speaking about what we have seen and heard." After threatening them again, they let them go, finding no way to punish them because of the people, for all of them praised God for what had happened. For the man on whom this sign of healing had been performed was more than forty years old.

Acts 4:13-22

A Second Pentecost

When Peter and John were released from prison, they went immediately to the place where the Christians were gathered, knowing they would receive welcome and support. (Prisoners who are released today have the same need.) The community listened eagerly to all that had happened. Then together they prayed over the news. It is interesting to note how they prayed. Their prayer began with a reflection on what had just happened, which connected it with both the Old Testament and the life of Jesus. Scriptural prayer is learning to find ourselves in the biblical text. This is what they were doing.

After this reflection the prayer moved on to petition. At this time of crisis, they did not pray for the removal of the difficulties that surrounded them, but for that boldness the Spirit gives to continue witnessing to Jesus, in spite of the difficulties.

Their prayer was answered by a second Pentecost experience. God saw that the little community needed a new outpouring of the Spirit in the face of persecution. Again the whole house was shaken and they were filled with the Holy Spirit so that they spoke the word of God with boldness. The Spirit will shake the church up frequently throughout history. Pentecost was not a once-for-all event.

After they were released, they went to their friends and reported what the chief priests and the elders had said to them. When they heard it, they raised their voices together to God and said, "Sovereign Lord, who made the heaven and the earth, the sea, and everything in them, it is you who said by the Holy Spirit through our ancestor David, your servant:

'Why did the Gentiles rage,
and the peoples imagine vain things?
The kings of the earth took their stand,
and the rulers have gathered together against
the Lord and against his Messiah.'

For in this city, in fact, both Herod and Pontius Pilate, with the Gentiles and the peoples of Israel, gathered together against your holy servant Jesus, whom you anointed, to do whatever your hand and your plan had predestined to take place. And now, Lord, look at their threats, and grant to your servants to speak your word with all boldness, while you stretch out your hand to heal, and signs and wonders are performed through the name of your holy servant Jesus." When they had prayed, the place in which they were gathered together was shaken; and they were all filled with the Holy Spirit and spoke the word of God with boldness.

Acts 4:23-31

—⁓—

Community Created by the Spirit

The coming of the Spirit created a unique kind of community among the believers. They shared their lives and their possessions as well as their faith. These were people of different social classes, who would probably have had no contact with each other if the Spirit had not drawn them together. Wealthy members sold their property and entrusted the proceeds to the apostles. There were no strings attached. They did not give as we ordinarily do, a little here and a little there as we like, keeping the poor forever dependent on us.

One man who turned everything over to the apostles is particularly mentioned by Luke because he will be important later in the story: Joseph, who was renamed Barnabas. Luke also explains that the new name given to Joseph by the apostles means "son of encouragement." When Paul enters the story later, we will see how appropriate this name was.

> Now the whole group of those who believed were of one heart and soul, and no one claimed private ownership of any possessions, but everything they owned was held in common. With great power the apostles gave their testimony to the resurrection of the Lord Jesus, and great grace was upon them all. There was not a needy person among them, for as many as owned lands or houses sold them and brought the proceeds of what was sold. They laid it at the apostles' feet, and it was distributed to each as any had need. There was a Levite, a native of Cyprus, Joseph, to whom the apostles gave the name Barnabas (which means "son of encouragement"). He sold a field that belonged to him, then brought the money, and laid it at the apostles' feet.

Acts 4:32-37

—*m*—

Growth and Persecution

Others must have been attracted to the infant Church by the witness of their community life as well as the boldness of their preaching. They were also drawn by the many cures worked by the apostles, like those worked by Jesus. What Peter and John began was now carried on by the whole team.

> Now many signs and wonders were done among the people through the apostles. And they were all together in Solomon's Portico. None of the rest dared to join them, but the people held them in high esteem. Yet more than ever believers were added to the Lord, great numbers of both men and women, so that they even carried out the sick into the streets, and laid them on cots and mats, in order that Peter's shadow might fall on some of them as he came by. A great number of people would also gather from the towns around Jerusalem, bringing the sick and those tormented by unclean spirits, and they were all cured.

Acts 5:12-16

All these healings and conversions were threatening to the established religious leaders. They arrested the apostles again. But during the night an angel let them out of prison and instructed them to continue preaching. (Luke gives angels an important place in both the story of the infant Jesus and that of the infant church.) At dawn the next day the apostles were in the temple evangelizing.

Luke enjoys the humor of the next scene. He paints it vividly. The high priest calls together all the elders and leaders of the people for a full-scale trial with which to settle once and for all this troublesome business of the followers of Jesus. When they are gathered in solemn assembly, the high priest sends policemen to bring the culprits. The policemen return embarrassed. The prison was properly locked, they report, but the prisoners were not there! There is consternation in the courtroom. Soon someone arrives to tell the disconcerted authorities that the men they are looking for are at that moment preaching in the temple.

The police are sent to arrest them again. The high priest scolds the apostles roundly for boldly continuing their preaching after being forbidden to do so. Their reply is one Christians throughout the ages have often had to make: "We must obey God rather than any human authority."

Then the high priest took action; he and all who were with him (that is, the sect of the Sadducees), being filled with jealousy, arrested the apostles and put them in the public prison. But during the night an angel of the Lord opened the prison doors, brought them out, and said, "Go, stand in the temple and tell the people the whole message about this life." When they heard this, they entered the temple at daybreak and went on with their teaching.

When the high priest and those with him arrived, they called together the council and the whole body of the elders of Israel, and sent to the prison to have them brought. But when the temple police went there, they did not find them in the prison; so they returned and reported, "We found the prison securely locked and the guards standing at the doors, but when we opened them, we found no one inside." Now when the captain of the temple and the chief priests heard these words, they were perplexed about them, wondering what might be going on. Then someone arrived and announced, "Look, the men whom you put in prison are standing in the temple and teaching the people!" Then the captain went with the temple police and brought them, but without violence, for they were afraid of being stoned by the people.

When they had brought them, they had them stand before the council. The high priest questioned them, saying, "We gave you strict orders not to teach in this name, yet here you have filled Jerusalem with your teaching and you are determined to bring this man's blood on us." But

Peter and the apostles answered, "We must obey God rather than any human authority. The God of our ancestors raised up Jesus, whom you had killed by hanging him on a tree. God exalted him at his right hand as Leader and Savior that he might give repentance to Israel and forgiveness of sins. And we are witnesses to these things, and so is the Holy Spirit whom God has given to those who obey him."

Acts 5:17-32

—∿—

A Wise Elder Intervenes

The message about Jesus, which attracted so many of the ordinary Jews, enraged the authorities so much that they wanted to kill the apostles. But there was one wise elder in the council named Gamaliel. He had learned from experience not to judge quickly. It is only from the experience of a lifetime that we learn how little we know. This single brave man persuaded the enraged group not to kill the apostles. They only flogged and ordered them again not to preach about Jesus. The authorities looked a bit silly at this point. It is evident that their orders would not be obeyed.

The apostles rejoiced at their suffering for the cause of Jesus. This will be the characteristic of Christian martyrs of all times. Perhaps their joy was the most striking part of their witness, as is the joy of Christians who suffer today in all kinds of situations. The joy that permeates Luke's account of the infancy of Jesus also permeates his account of the infancy of the church, even during difficult times.

When [the council] heard this, they were enraged and wanted to kill them. But a Pharisee in the council named Gamaliel, a teacher of the law, respected by all the people, stood up and ordered the men to be put outside for a short time. Then he said to them, "Fellow Israelites, consider carefully what you propose to do to these men. For some time ago Theudas rose up, claiming to be somebody, and a number of men, about four hundred, joined him; but he was killed, and all who followed him were dispersed and disappeared. After him Judas the Galilean rose up at the time of the census and got people to follow him; he also perished, and all who followed him were scattered. So in the present case, I tell you, keep away from these men and let them alone; because if this plan or this undertaking is of human origin, it will fail; but if it is of God, you will not be able to overthrow them—in that case you may even be found fighting against God!"

They were convinced by him, and when they had called in the apostles, they had them flogged. Then they ordered them not to speak in the name of Jesus, and let them go. As they left the council, they rejoiced that they were considered worthy to suffer dishonor for the sake of the name. And every day in the temple and at home they did not cease to teach and proclaim Jesus as the Messiah.

Acts 5:33-42

—⁓—

Questions for Reflection

1. How do you imagine the life of the cripple and his family would have changed after his healing? Might some of the changes have been difficult?

2. Peter empowered the cripple. What are some ways in which we can empower those in need, even if we cannot work miracles?

3. What situation do you know when someone was open to hearing about Jesus because of seeing the effects of Jesus in another person's life?

4. Can you think of someone who experienced a healing or conversion after the age of forty? Do you expect new and exciting things to happen in your life?

5. What situation can you think of in which someone has to choose whether to obey God or a human authority?

6. How could modern Christians be more like these: "There was no needy person among them, for those who owned property or houses would sell them, bring the proceeds of the sale, and put them at the feet of the apostles" (Acts 4:34).

7. Can you think of a situation where the wisdom of Gamaliel might be useful: "...keep away from these men and let them alone; because if this...undertaking is of human origin it will fail; but if it is of God, you will not be able to overthrow them..." (Acts 5:42)?

Suggestion for Further Reading
Acts 3-5

CHAPTER FIFTEEN

The Seven

Meeting the Needs of Widows

AS DISCUSSED EARLIER, THROUGHOUT THE BIBLE, widows are thought of as the typical poor people. In biblical society there were no career women, and a woman without a man to support and protect her was extremely vulnerable. For that reason God always called the Israelites to special concern for widows. The early Christians continued this tradition. This is not irrelevant to our times, as statistics show that, worldwide, widows are still at the bottom of the economic ladder.

The early Christians remembered that the good news about Jesus was first proclaimed by the widow Anna who saw the child at his presentation in the temple (Luke 2:36-38). And they remembered the special concern Jesus showed for the widow of Nain (Luke 7:11-17) and his admiration for the widow who contributed two pennies to the temple treasury—all she had (Luke 21:1-4).

If all widows were vulnerable, widows from minority groups were more so. A minority that does not speak the language of the majority is the most vulnerable of all. In Jerusalem, the majority spoke Aramaic, a dialect of Hebrew, but many Jews who had lived their lives elsewhere but retired in Jerusalem spoke Greek. If the husband died, his wife was left alone—far from her children in a land whose language she did not know. To the natives of Jerusalem, she would be a poor and elderly immigrant, a strain on the welfare system.

Both Greek-speaking and Hebrew-speaking Jews were caught up in the enthusiasm of Pentecost and joined the infant church. The Spirit did not blot out differences of language and culture or the subtle discrimination that might arise from them. Members of the Greek-speaking, or Hellenist, group within the church protested bitterly that their widows were not being provided for as the Hebrew-speaking widows were. It was not so different from many protests we hear today from minority groups.

The apostles listened to the complaints carefully. They realized that they could not deal with the issue alone, so they called the whole community together and presented the problem. They also proposed a solution. Because the responsibilities of leading the growing community had become too much for the twelve of them, they proposed that some of their responsibilities be delegated to others.

The community agreed and selected seven men to fill this new role. The men selected by the community were then presented to the apostles, who commissioned them by a laying on of hands. This is an interesting decision-making process, in which the minority protesters, the leaders and the entire assembly all participate in different ways. The result is an expanded staff for the first Christian parish and, presumably, fair treatment for the minority poor.

Of the seven new staff members, Stephen is mentioned first and with special emphasis because he will be important later in the story.

> Now during those days, when the disciples were increasing in number, the Hellenists complained against the Hebrews because their widows were being neglected in the daily distribution of food. And the twelve called together the whole community of the disciples and said, "It is not right that we should neglect the word of God in order to wait on tables. Therefore, friends, select from among yourselves seven men of good standing, full of the Spirit and of wisdom, whom we may appoint to this task, while we, for our part, will devote ourselves to prayer and to serving the word." What they said pleased the whole community, and they chose Stephen, a man full of faith and the Holy Spirit, together with Philip, Prochorus, Nicanor, Timon, Parmenas, and Nicolaus, a proselyte of Antioch.

They had these men stand before the apostles, who prayed
and laid their hands on them.

Acts 6:1-6

~~~

The Passion of Stephen

Luke now focuses on one of these newly delegated helpers,
Stephen. His ministry soon reached beyond serving the widows into the working of miracles and preaching. It is hard to
corral a person filled with the Spirit into a job description!
When some of the Hellenist Jews could not beat him in argument, they started false rumors about him that upset the
elders and scribes, those with a big investment in the religious status quo. Like Jesus, Stephen was accused of disregard
for the current religious structures: the temple and the law. It
was said that he wanted to change the sacred customs that
went back to the time of Moses. It is a familiar complaint. The
customs in question may well go back no further than the
lifetime of the complainer. It is a complaint of people who are
threatened by the new.

On the basis of these false charges he is brought to trial
before the high priest. He defends himself with a long
speech reminding his hearers what history really teaches:
God was always present with Israel, but showed little interest in the temple or other religious structures so precious
to many people. Stephen is trying to give perspective on
Jesus by putting him in the broader context of Jewish history. If these people who referred to history so glibly just
studied it carefully they would change their views drasti-
cally! We will read only the ending of this speech, in which
Stephen accuses his hearers of opposing the Holy Spirit
just as their ancestors had. Like Peter, he blames them very
specifically for the murder of Jesus.

Stephen, full of grace and power, did great wonders and
signs among the people. Then some of those who

belonged to the synagogue of the Freedmen (as it was called), Cyrenians, Alexandrians, and others of those from Cilicia and Asia, stood up and argued with Stephen. But they could not withstand the wisdom and the Spirit with which he spoke. Then they secretly instigated some men to say, "We have heard him speak blasphemous words against Moses and God." They stirred up the people as well as the elders and the scribes; then they suddenly confronted him, seized him, and brought him before the council. They set up false witnesses who said, "This man never stops saying things against this holy place and the law; for we have heard him say that this Jesus of Nazareth will destroy this place and will change the customs that Moses handed on to us." And all who sat in the council looked intently at him, and they saw that his face was like the face of an angel. . . .

[Stephen said] "You stiff-necked people, uncircumcised in heart and ears, you are forever opposing the Holy Spirit, just as your ancestors used to do. Which of the prophets did your ancestors not persecute? They killed those who foretold the coming of the Righteous One, and now you have become his betrayers and murderers. You are the ones that received the law as ordained by angels, and yet you have not kept it."

Acts 6:8-15; 7:51-53

—⁓—

The mob was infuriated by Stephen's speech. Luke draws a vivid contrast between their frenzy and Stephen's sacred calm as they stone him to death. We see another of the fruits of Pentecost when we read that Stephen was filled with the Holy Spirit as he was dragged to his death. His final words are like Jesus': "Lord Jesus, receive my spirit," and "Lord, do not hold this sin against them." They bring him outside the city for the gruesome proceedings, as Jesus had been crucified outside the city.

A young man named Saul saw all of this. It entered his

soul like a time bomb. It would have no immediate visible effect. He would continue persecuting the Christians, in fact more fiercely than before. Later, the example and the prayer of Stephen would turn him into the great apostle Paul.

> When they heard these things, they became enraged and ground their teeth at Stephen. But filled with the Holy Spirit, he gazed into heaven and saw the glory of God and Jesus standing at the right hand of God. "Look," he said, "I see the heavens opened and the Son of Man standing at the right hand of God!" But they covered their ears, and with a loud shout all rushed together against him. Then they dragged him out of the city and began to stone him; and the witnesses laid their coats at the feet of a young man named Saul. While they were stoning Stephen, he prayed, "Lord Jesus, receive my spirit." Then he knelt down and cried out in a loud voice, "Lord, do not hold this sin against them." When he had said this, he died.
> And Saul approved of their killing him.

> *Acts 7:54-60; 8:1*

Philip and the Samaritans

After the martyrdom of Stephen, a severe persecution broke out against Christian men and women. What Paul and the other persecutors never guessed was that God would use their persecution as a way of spreading the gospel. Christians fleeing the persecution brought the gospel wherever they went, leading the church to a transition that might never have happened if they had stayed in Jerusalem.

Philip, one of the seven newly commissioned assistants, went to Samaria. The Jews thought of the Samaritans as schismatics and despised them even more than they did the Gentiles. This split between the Samaritans, who were the remnant of the ten northern tribes, and the Jews went back to the death of Solomon (1 Kings 12:1-20). It had all the bitterness of a family feud. The early Jewish Christians had to become reconciled with the Samaritans before they would be ready to reach out to the Gentiles.

Philip brought the joy of the gospel to the Samaritans, and he baptized them. Surprisingly, the manifestations of the Spirit which usually accompanied baptism did not occur in the case of these Samaritans. This is one of several places where Luke is showing how unpredictable are the ways of God. We cannot observe the usual divine pattern and turn it into a rule as if God always has to act in the same way.

The apostles in Jerusalem heard about the great missionary work of Philip, but also about the surprising absence of visible signs of the Spirit. They sent Peter and John to complete the work that Philip had begun so well. It is a little surprising to see the first leader of the church sent on an errand by his fellow apostles!

We do not know how Peter and John felt about the assignment. When they had come to Samaria with Jesus they had not been welcomed, and John had suggested to Jesus that he send down fire from heaven on the nasty Samaritans (Luke 9:54). Only Luke's Gospel tells that story. Perhaps it interested him as a preparation for this story.

The mission to Samaria is an example of collaboration between the Philip the initiator, the community in Jerusalem, and their delegates, Peter and John.

That day a severe persecution began against the church in Jerusalem, and all except the apostles were scattered throughout the countryside of Judea and Samaria. Devout men buried Stephen and made loud lamentation over him. But Saul was ravaging the church by entering house after house; dragging off both men and women, he committed them to prison.

Now those who were scattered went from place to place, proclaiming the word. Philip went down to the city of Samaria and proclaimed the Messiah to them. The crowds with one accord listened eagerly to what was said by Philip, hearing and seeing the signs that he did, for unclean spirits, crying with loud shrieks, came out of many who were possessed; and many others who were paralyzed or lame were cured. So there was great joy in that city.

Now when the apostles at Jerusalem heard that Samaria had accepted the word of God, they sent Peter and John to them. The two went down and prayed for them that they might receive the Holy Spirit (for as yet the Spirit had not come upon any of them; they had only been baptized in the name of the Lord Jesus). Then Peter and John laid their hands on them, and they received the Holy Spirit.

Acts 8:1-8; 14-17

Philip and the Ethiopian Eunuch

If Jews disliked Samaritans, they were disgusted by eunuchs. In other countries of the Ancient Near East it was common to castrate men intended for service in the king's court, especially in his harem. Jews who were forcibly subjected to this operation felt it a terrible disgrace. They were not permitted into the temple (Deuteronomy 23:2). One of the most extraordinary promises of the prophet Isaiah was that one day there would be a place even for eunuchs among God's people (Isaiah 56:3-5). Sexual abnormality made a person an outcast.

This eunuch was a black man, from far away Ethiopia. He was on a spiritual journey, so hungry for God that he made the long trip to the Jerusalem temple even though he knew he would not be permitted inside it to worship. He experienced what many pilgrims today experience. He did find what he was seeking on his journey but not in the place or way he had anticipated.

He thought his pilgrimage was over, and he was sitting in his chariot on his way home, reading the prophet Isaiah. As was customary among ancient people, he read aloud.

Philip, who had been instructed by an angel to walk along the same road, heard him reading and asked him if he understood what he was reading. He was humble enough to admit that he needed help to interpret the passage, and Phillip used this as a beginning point for preaching the gospel to him. Almost any point where a seeker has a question can be an opening for evangelization.

The eunuch believed and was baptized and went on his way rejoicing like the Samaritans. Through him the gospel spread into Africa before it came to Europe!

Ethiopian Christians even today have a special love for Jerusalem. "Jerusalem" is a popular name of Christian women in Ethiopia today. Ethiopian monks have a tiny chapel on the roof of the Church of the Holy Sepulcher in Jerusalem. When I came there with a pilgrim group the monk on duty welcomed us warmly and solemnly picked up a book of Scripture in the shape of a cross. He read from it, in his own language, the story of the Ethiopian eunuch.

After his encounter with the Ethiopian, Philip preached the gospel in many towns, ending in Caesarea, a place that will be important as our story develops.

Then an angel of the Lord said to Philip, "Get up and go toward the south to the road that goes down from Jerusalem to Gaza." (This is a wilderness road.) So he got up and went. Now there was an Ethiopian eunuch, a court official of the Candace, queen of the Ethiopians, in charge of her entire treasury. He had come to Jerusalem to worship and was returning home; seated in his chariot, he was reading the prophet Isaiah. Then the Spirit said to Philip, "Go over to this chariot and join it." So Philip ran up to it and heard him reading the prophet Isaiah. He asked, "Do you understand what you are reading?" He replied, "How can I, unless someone guides me?" And he invited Philip to get in and sit beside him. Now the passage of the Scripture that he was reading was this: "Like a sheep he was led to the slaughter, and like a lamb silent before its shearer, so he does not open his mouth. In his humiliation justice was denied him. Who can describe his generation? For his life is taken away from the earth." The eunuch asked Philip, "About whom, may I ask you, does the prophet say this, about himself or about someone else?" Then Philip began to speak, and starting with this Scripture, he proclaimed to him the good news about Jesus. As they were going along the road, they came to some water; and the eunuch said, "Look, here is water! What is to prevent me from being baptized?" He commanded the chariot to stop, and both of them, Philip and the eunuch, went down into the water, and Philip baptized him. When they came up out of the water, the Spirit of the Lord snatched Philip away; the eunuch saw him no more, and went on his way rejoicing. But Philip found himself at Azotus, and as he was passing through the region, he proclaimed the good news to all the towns until he came to Caesarea.

Acts 8:26-40

Questions for Reflection

1. Do you think the church today provides for the needs of widows as well as the early church did?

2. Because the apostles could not do everything, they delegated some responsibilities to the seven. Does anything similar happen in your church? Would you like it to happen more often than it does?

3. Stephen's death expressed the meaning of his whole life. Is this true of anyone you know?

4. Stephen's last act was to forgive his murderers. Do you know of anyone who forgave enemies before death?

5. In our country, what groups are looked down on, as Samaritans were looked down on by Jews? Who serves the spiritual needs of these people as Philip and Peter and John served those of the Samaritans?

6. Can you think of an apparently accidental encounter, like that of Philip and the Ethiopian, that in retrospect seemed to show the providence of God?

Suggestion for Further Reading
Acts 6-8

CHAPTER SIXTEEN

The Conversion of Paul

The Road to Damascus

WHEN THE ELDERS OF THE FIRST CHRISTIAN community met, they must have shaken their heads over that young fanatic Saul, who broke into the homes of Christians and tied up both men and women to bring them to prison. He even obtained authorization to travel to Damascus in Syria to expand the violent persecution. This was a young man who had received the best education Jerusalem had to offer, yet he was behaving like a madman. Violent youth are not just a modern phenomenon.

The first Christians preached boldly and made thousands of converts, but this young hellion was too much for even their powers of persuasion. Jesus himself would have to intervene to change Saul's direction. Actually, Saul was not a bad person. He believed in the Scriptures. He was a Pharisee. Pharisees were zealous observers of the law. Some were truly religious people. Their temptation was to be too sure of their own righteousness, much like the Pharisee in Jesus' parable who piously thanked God that he was not like the sinful tax collector (Luke 18:9). Paul was zealous in what he saw as the service of God. But the zeal of youth, without the wisdom that comes with long experience and many humiliations, can be destructive.

However, the young man who appeared to be a lost cause was not. As Saul was traveling to Damascus, full of righteous rage against those following the new way of Jesus, Jesus himself struck him to the ground. This violent young man needed to be approached violently. Yet once Jesus had Saul's attention, he spoke to him plaintively, "Saul, Saul, why do you persecute me?" These words were burned into Saul's heart and much later gave birth to his profound theology of the identification of every Christian with Jesus. It is because Christ lives in every Christian that whatever is done to a Christian is done to Christ.

The conceited young man was devastated and blinded by his experience of Jesus. He limped into the city, led by the hand by one of his companions. What a contrast to the fiery entrance into the city he had anticipated! For three days he sat, blind and stunned, unable to eat or drink. His physical strength had left him along with his certainty of his righteousness.

> Meanwhile Saul, still breathing threats and murder against the disciples of the Lord, went to the high priest and asked him for letters to the synagogues at Damascus, so that if he found any who belonged to the Way, men or women, he might bring them bound to Jerusalem. Now as he was going along and approaching Damascus, suddenly a light from heaven flashed around him. He fell to the ground and heard a voice saying to him, "Saul, Saul, why do you persecute me?" He asked, "Who are you, Lord?" The reply came, "I am Jesus, whom you are persecuting. But get up and enter the city, and you will be told what you are to do." The men who were traveling with him stood speechless because they heard the voice but saw no one. Saul got up from the ground, and though his eyes were open, he could see nothing; so they led him by the hand and brought him into Damascus. For three days he was without sight, and neither ate nor drank.

Acts 9:1-9

Ananias

There was a Christian in Damascus named Ananias. He was not a particularly important person; we know nothing about him except what we find in this story. But his role was to serve as Saul's mentor. Often the major characters in the biblical story could not have accomplished anything if some minor character had not been there for them at the time when they needed help.

God speaks to Ananias in a vision, telling him to visit Saul. Ananias, who is no fool, informs the Lord that this is not a good plan. He has information about this Saul which the Almighty seems not to have. God replies in one of the great non-sequiturs of divine dialogue. He does not deny Ananias' information, but adds some new and unlikely information. This Saul is to bring the name of Jesus to Gentiles and Jews, and to suffer much in doing it. Ananias knows when he is outranked, so he goes to visit Saul.

He finds Saul blind and in a state of shock, but praying. Traumatic experiences can be a great incentive to prayer. Then Ananias, who had been so afraid of this fiery persecutor, greets him in a surprising way. "Brother Saul . . . " For the Christian, every creature of God is brother or sister, even those who threaten everything we hold dear. Then he lays hands on him, that ancient liturgical gesture, and baptizes him. Scales fall from Saul's eyes, as they are no doubt falling from the eyes of his heart. Then the Holy Spirit comes upon him, as it came on the disciples at Pentecost.

Saul's conversion is a reminder to us that conversion is the work of the Lord, yet once God has done the major part, the person beginning a Christian life needs the ministry of other Christians. These others may be people much less spiritually gifted than the new convert.

Now there was a disciple in Damascus named Ananias. The Lord said to him in a vision, "Ananias." He answered, "Here I am, Lord." The Lord said to him, "Get up and go to the street called Straight, and at the house of Judas look for a man of Tarsus named Saul. At this moment he is praying, and he has seen in a vision a man named Ananias come in and lay his hands on him so that he might regain his sight." But Ananias answered, "Lord, I have heard from many about this man, how much evil he has done to your saints in

Jerusalem; and here he has authority from the chief priests to bind all who invoke your name." But the Lord said to him, "Go, for he is an instrument whom I have chosen to bring my name before Gentiles and kings and before the people of Israel; I myself will show him how much he must suffer for the sake of my name." So Ananias went and entered the house. He laid his hands on Saul and said, "Brother Saul, the Lord Jesus, who appeared to you on your way here, has sent me so that you may regain your sight and be filled with the Holy Spirit." And immediately something like scales fell from his eyes, and his sight was restored. Then he got up and was baptized, and after taking some food, he regained his strength.

Acts 9:10-19

—⁓—

The New Convert

Saul was like many new converts, so full of his extraordinary conversion experience that he shared it with everyone. The Jews of Damascus, knowing why he had come there, were amazed. We are not told that he made many converts as the Jerusalem community had, but he surely made an impression: such a powerful impression that the Jews tried to kill him.

He reminds us of the young Moses, who was so enthusiastic about the liberation of his people that he appointed himself mediator among them and killed an Egyptian. All of this accomplished nothing for the people. Moses had to flee and spent forty years in exile in the desert, growing up. When he had matured, God called him to that same work of the liberation of his people, and he succeeded beyond all human possibility. Saul, too, would need time in exile to mature before his extraordinarily fruitful ministry could begin.

In the relative failure of his first mission, Saul was not only like Moses but also like Jesus, whose first recorded sermon stirred up the people of Nazareth to violence against him (Luke 4:16–30). Like Saul, Jesus escaped, to continue his ministry more fruitfully elsewhere.

Later, in his letter to the Corinthians (2 Corinthians 11:32, 33), Paul would remember the humiliating end of his self-appointed evangelism in Damascus. So much hostility arose against him that he had to escape the city hidden in a basket!

> For several days he was with the disciples in Damascus, and immediately he began to proclaim Jesus in the synagogues, saying, "He is the Son of God." All who heard him were amazed and said, "Is not this the man who made havoc in Jerusalem among those who invoked this name? And has he not come here for the purpose of bringing them bound before the chief priests?" Saul became increasingly more powerful and confounded the Jews who lived in Damascus by proving that Jesus was the Messiah. After some time had passed, the Jews plotted to kill him, but their plot became known to Saul. They were watching the gates day and night so that they might kill him; but his disciples took him by night and let him down through an opening in the wall, lowering him in a basket.

Acts 9:19b–25

Barnabas

After his failure in Damascus, Saul returned to Jerusalem. Christians there had vivid memories of him breaking into their homes, arresting them and bringing them to prison. It is not easy for frightened people to accept a former enemy into their community.

As in the case of Ananias, it was a relatively unimportant member of the Christian community, Barnabas, who was able to bring Saul into the community in spite of his past. Now we see why in Chapter Four the Levite Joseph, who sold his property and contributed the proceeds to the apostles, was given the name Barnabas, which means "son of encouragement." People like him, who can encourage those on the periphery and link them with the community, render a great service, even if they themselves never come into the spotlight.

Once accepted by the Christian community, Saul preached boldly, like the apostles. He continued the special ministry to the Hellenists which Stephen had begun. He must often have remembered his role in the stoning of Stephen.

Saul was bold, but perhaps not yet wise. He argued vehemently but aroused more hostility than conversion. As in Damascus, he became too hot to handle, and the Christian community arranged for him to go to the closest seaport, Caesarea, to return to his hometown of Tarsus, in what we today call Turkey. During his years of apparent inactivity there, God was preparing him for his real mission.

> When he had come to Jerusalem, he attempted to join the disciples; and they were all afraid of him, for they did not believe that he was a disciple. But Barnabas took him, brought him to the apostles, and described for them how on the road he had seen the Lord, who had spoken to him, and how in Damascus he had spoken boldly in the name of Jesus. So he went in and out among them in Jerusalem, speaking boldly in the name of the Lord. He spoke and argued with the Hellenists; but they were attempting to kill him. When the believers learned of it, they brought him down to Caesarea and sent him off to Tarsus.

Acts 9:26-30

Aeneas and Dorcas

The scene shifts from Paul back to Peter, who is traveling around the Holy Land, visiting the churches there. With Paul out of the way, there is an interval of peace for the Church. Luke tells two stories of events that happened during this time to allow his readers to catch their breaths between the dramatic account of the conversion of Saul and the equally dramatic account of the conversion of Peter, which is coming.

As he often does, Luke puts two parallel stories side by side, one about a man and the other about a woman. When he paralleled the stories of Simeon and Anna, that of Simeon was more developed. In this case, the story of the woman is much more fully developed.

In the first story, Peter visited the church in Lydda. This is modern Lod, site of the airport which serves both Jerusalem and Tel Aviv. There he healed a man named Aeneas, who had been paralyzed for eight years. As people in Jerusalem were brought to faith by the sight of the blind man who was cured, the people of the area around Lydda believed in Jesus because they saw the paralyzed man who was cured.

> Now as Peter went here and there among all the believers, he came down also to the saints living in Lydda. There he found a man named Aeneas, who had been bedridden for eight years, for he was paralyzed. Peter said to him, "Aeneas, Jesus Christ heals you; get up and make your bed!" And immediately he got up. And all the residents of Lydda and Sharon saw him and turned to the Lord.

Acts 9:32-35

While Peter was in Lydda, he received a message from the Christians in nearby Joppa, modern Jaffa. They needed his pastoral presence because an important member of their community had died, Dorcas. (She is also called Tabitha. Both names mean "gazelle.") Dorcas played the role in the Joppa community for which the seven were chosen in the Jerusalem community. She provided for the needs of the widows.

In a culture where women lived their social lives quite separate from men, we get a glimpse of a community of

Christian women in this story. All the widows stood around the body of their friend Dorcas, weeping and showing off with reverence the clothing she had woven and sewn for them. It is clear that Dorcas, a woman of some means, used her resources as well as her time to provide for other women who could not provide for themselves. There is a Christian nursing home in Nebraska called "The Tabitha Home," a reminder of the Christian women over the centuries who have continued the work of Dorcas.

Peter quickly made the ten-mile journey to Joppa and went up to the room where the widows surrounded the body of their beloved Dorcas. Perhaps he remembered the time he, James and John, had come with Jesus into another room where a woman, much younger that time, lay dead, surrounded by much weeping. That was the daughter of Jairus. Jesus had taken her by the hand, saying, "Child, get up!" (Luke 8:40–56). Peter knew that Jesus continued to work through him. He said, "Tabitha, get up!" and took her by the hand, helping her to rise.

We are not surprised to hear that many in the area around Joppa came to believe when they saw Dorcas alive and continuing her ministry to the widows.

> Now in Joppa there was a disciple whose name was Tabitha, which in Greek is Dorcas. She was devoted to good works and acts of charity. At that time she became ill and died. When they had washed her, they laid her in a room upstairs. Since Lydda was near Joppa, the disciples, who heard that Peter was there, sent two men to him with the request, "Please come to us without delay." So Peter got up and went with them; and when he arrived, they took him to the room upstairs. All the widows stood beside him, weeping and showing tunics and other clothing that Dorcas had made while she was with them. Peter put all of them outside, and then he knelt down and prayed. He turned to the body and said, "Tabitha, get up." Then she opened her eyes, and seeing Peter, she sat up. He gave her his hand and helped her up. Then calling the saints and

widows, he showed her to be alive. This became known throughout Joppa, and many believed in the Lord.

Acts 9:36-42

Questions for Reflection

1. Do you know any young people today who remind you of Saul during his fanatic and violent period?

2. Do you know any story besides Saul's of a surprising conversion?

3. Do you know of a seasoned Christian like Ananias who is able to help those in crisis? What qualities make a person suitable for such a responsibility?

4. Why do you think a period of blindness and inaction was part of Saul's conversion process?

5. Do you know someone like Barnabas who serves a community by welcoming newcomers and helping old timers to accept them? How could you be like Barnabas?

6. Dorcas made it her responsibility to care for needy widows. Do you know individuals or groups that take on this responsibility today? How can you help to care for widows and other needy persons in your community?

Suggestions for Further Reading
Acts 9:1-43; Galatians 1:11-24; Luke 8:40-56

CHAPTER SEVENTEEN

The Conversion of Peter

Cornelius

WE COME NOW TO A STORY THAT WAS VERY important for Luke. We know that because it is the longest story he tells, and he tells it three times. The story is about a very interesting character, Cornelius. Cornelius was a centurion, an important officer in the Roman army. As such, he represented everything the Jews despised: paganism, foreignness and the oppressive military power of Rome. He was not only not part of God's chosen people, he was part of the hostile force that occupied their country.

On the other hand, this centurion was a God-fearer, one of those Gentiles who lived on the fringes of Judaism, respecting its religious values, worshiping in the synagogues, but not circumcised or observant of the laws of purity that controlled every detail of a Jew's daily life. He was a kind of bridge figure, standing halfway between Jew and Gentile. He reminds us of the centurion in Capernaum, also a God-fearer and generous to Jewish causes, whose servant Jesus cured (Luke 7:1–10).

This person who was a symbolic link between Judaism and the Gentile world lived in a very appropriate city, Caesarea. Caesarea was a magnificent port city built by Herod the Great. It was a "hub city" for Rome, through which their communication with the Jews passed. It was the most thoroughly Gentile city in Palestine. Pontius Pilate and other Roman authorities lived there. Jesus never visited it, and it is unlikely that observant Jews like the apostles did either.

Cornelius was praying at 3 P.M., a customary prayer time for Jews. An angel came with a strange message. Cornelius was to send men to Joppa, thirty miles away and find someone named Peter. The centurion obeyed without question.

In Caesarea there was a man named Cornelius, a centurion of the Italian Cohort, as it was called. He was a devout man who feared God with all his household; he gave alms generously to the people and prayed constantly to God. One afternoon at about three o'clock he had a vision in which he clearly saw an angel of God coming in and saying to him, "Cornelius." He stared at him in terror and said, "What is it, Lord?" He answered, "Your prayers and your alms have ascended as a memorial before God. Now send men to Joppa for a certain Simon who is called Peter; he is lodging with Simon, a tanner, whose house is by the seaside." When the angel who spoke to him had left, he called two of his slaves and a devout soldier from the ranks of those who served him, and after telling them everything, he sent them to Joppa.

Acts 10:1-8

Peter

In the story of the conversion of Paul, two people, Paul and Ananias, each had a vision, and the visions brought them together by the plan of God. In this story of the conversion of Peter, Peter and Cornelius each have a vision, and the visions bring them together by another plan of God.

Peter, like Cornelius, was at prayer when the vision occurred. His vision was even stranger than that of Cornelius. He saw something like a large sheet or tablecloth come down from heaven. It contained animals of every kind, including some that Jewish kosher law did not permit him to eat. He was hungry, and a voice invited him,

"Kill and eat." Like Ananias when he was told to go to Saul, Peter tried to argue with the Lord. Conscientious Jew that he was, Peter was shocked at the very idea of eating non-kosher food and reminded the Lord that he had a perfect record—he had never eaten anything forbidden by the law. The argument that "I have never done such a thing" does not impress the Lord very much. The Lord responds with a radical statement, one that will be central to the whole transition recorded in Acts. "What God has made clean, you must not call profane." God is telling Peter that the kosher food laws have been canceled. More importantly, the message is that the Gentiles, whom Jews always avoided as unclean, were now to be accepted by the Christian community. God is repealing God's own law.

> About noon the next day, as they were on their journey and approaching the city, Peter went up on the roof to pray. He became hungry and wanted something to eat; and while it was being prepared, he fell into a trance. He saw the heaven opened and something like a large sheet coming down, being lowered to the ground by its four corners. In it were all kinds of four-footed creatures and reptiles and birds of the air. Then he heard a voice saying, "Get up, Peter; kill and eat." But Peter said, "By no means, Lord; for I have never eaten anything that is profane or unclean." The voice said to him again, a second time, "What God has made clean, you must not call profane." This happened three times, and the thing was suddenly taken up to heaven.

Acts 10:9-16

Peter's Vision Explained

Peter must have been bewildered by the strange vision and the extraordinary words that went with it. But real life brought an immediate explanation. Three messengers from Cornelius arrived, telling Peter of Cornelius's vision. The two visions fit together, as sometimes two quite different insights can come together and make sense of each other.

For a Jew to offer hospitality to a Gentile was unheard of. Yet Peter invited these Gentile messengers into the Jewish home where he was a guest. Luke does not tell us how the owner of the house felt about it, but we can speculate that Simon the tanner, though Jewish, was more ready than other Jews for such a deviation from custom. Tanners were not allowed to live in towns because of the odors caused by the tanning process and the assumption that they were ritually impure because they handled skins of forbidden animals. By choosing to stay with a Jew looked down on by the Jewish community, Peter was already taking a step in the direction in which the Spirit was to propel him much further. Peter may have felt that the tanner was grateful enough for being accepted that he would accept even Gentiles into his house.

Peter agreed to return to Caesarea with the messengers. Knowing how shocking all this was to Jewish sensibilities, he took some witnesses with him from the Christian community at Joppa. He did not want to be alone in the risky venture on which the Spirit was propelling him.

> Now while Peter was greatly puzzled about what to make of the vision that he had seen, suddenly the men sent by Cornelius appeared. They were asking for Simon's house and were standing by the gate. They called out to ask whether Simon, who was called Peter, was staying there. While Peter was still thinking about the vision, the Spirit said to him, "Look, three men are searching for you. Now get up, go down, and go with them without hesitation; for I have sent them." So Peter went down to the men and said, "I am the one you are looking for; what is the reason for your coming?" They answered, "Cornelius, a centurion, an upright and God-fearing man, who is well spoken of by the whole Jewish nation, was directed by a holy angel to send for you to come to his house and to hear what you have to say." So Peter invited them in and gave them lodging.

The next day he got up and went with them, and some
of the believers from Joppa accompanied him.

Acts 10:17-23

Peter and Cornelius Meet

These Jewish Christians must have been nervous at what was
probably their first journey to Caesarea. When I visited the
very impressive remains of that city, famous for its temples
and Roman public buildings, I could imagine how uncom-
fortable they must have been walking the great paved streets
and entering the home of a Roman official.

Cornelius greeted them respectfully and invited Peter
to speak to his assembled family and friends. In this alien
environment, Peter proclaimed the extraordinary message
of his vision: "God has shown me that I should not call anyone profane or unclean." There are a great many people
Jews considered unclean, in fact, everyone who was not an
observant Jew. Peter had done the same, but God converted him. He, and everyone around him, were as surprised as Paul and his friends were at his conversion.

The following day they came to Caesarea. Cornelius was
expecting them and had called together his relatives and
close friends. On Peter's arrival Cornelius met him, and
falling at his feet, worshiped him. But Peter made him get
up, saying, "Stand up; I am only a mortal." And as he talked
with him, he went in and found that many had assembled;
and he said to them, "You yourselves know that it is unlaw-
ful for a Jew to associate with or to visit a Gentile; but God
has shown me that I should not call anyone profane or
unclean. So when I was sent for, I came without objection.
Now may I ask why you sent for me?"

Acts 10:24-29

A Gentile Pentecost

Peter proclaimed the message of Jesus to the gathering in Cornelius's house, but before he could finish talking he was interrupted. The Spirit "fell upon" the audience in as dramatic a way as on the 120 disciples at the first Pentecost. They spoke in tongues and praised God.

Clearly, things were getting out of control. The Jewish Christians with Peter were astonished that the Holy Spirit would come on uncircumcised foreigners. To make matters worse, the Spirit had not observed the proper ritual procedure. Normally, converts were baptized and then received the Holy Spirit. In this case the Spirit came before water baptism. The Spirit was outrunning the church, and in a direction the members of the church had not planned. There was nothing for them to do but try to catch up by baptizing those on whom the Spirit had already come.

After this extraordinary experience, it seems an anticlimax to hear that the Jewish guests stayed for a few days at the home of Cornelius. Actually, it is quite an amazing statement. A day before they would not have dreamed of staying in a Gentile home where kosher food would not be available.

This event was a turning point in the life of the early Church as it went through its painful transition from being a group within Judaism to being a Gentile church independent of the synagogue. It would be remembered at the crucial Council of Jerusalem.

Then Peter began to speak to them: "I truly understand that God shows no partiality, but in every nation anyone who fears him and does what is right is acceptable to him. You know the message he sent to the people of Israel, preaching peace by Jesus Christ—he is Lord of all. That message spread throughout Judea, beginning in Galilee after the baptism that John announced: how God anointed Jesus of Nazareth with the Holy Spirit and with power; how he went about doing good and healing all who were oppressed by the devil, for God was with him. We are witnesses to all that he did both in Judea and in Jerusalem. They put him to death by hanging him on a tree; but God raised him on the third day and allowed him to appear, not to all the people but to us who were chosen by God as witnesses, and who ate and drank with him after he rose from the dead.

While Peter was still speaking, the Holy Spirit fell upon all who heard the word. The circumcised believers who had come with Peter were astounded that the gift of the Holy Spirit had been poured out even on the Gentiles, for they heard them speaking in tongues and extolling God. Then Peter said, "Can anyone withhold the water for baptizing these people who have received the Holy Spirit just as we have?" So he ordered them to be baptized in the name of Jesus Christ. Then they invited him to stay for several days.

Acts 10:34-41; 44-48

New Directions

We have seen Peter, the leader of the Christian community, taking a radical new direction. Now we see that the movement out to Gentiles is also a grassroots movement. (And it is the grassroots mission that will bear fruit throughout the rest of the story; Cornelius makes his point, then disappears from Acts.) Many lay Christians fled from the persecution in Jerusalem, bringing the new faith wherever they went. Today's lay missionaries are nothing new. "The Decree on the Apostolate of Lay People" of Vatican II refers to this passage in Acts when it says, "The Church can never be without the lay apostolate; it is something that derives from the layman's very vocation as a Christian. Scripture clearly shows how spontaneous and fruitful was this activity in the Church's early days"(P1).

A few unconventional individuals among these lay missionaries even had the audacity to preach to Gentiles! A great number were converted. When word about these extraordinary goings-on reached the mother church in Jerusalem, they sent Barnabas to Antioch to investigate.

The special open-mindedness of Barnabas which we noticed when he introduced Saul to the very suspicious Jerusalem community surfaces again here. When Barnabas sees the work of the Spirit among the Gentile converts he rejoices. Again he is a bridge person: this time between the Jerusalem community and the very different community in Antioch.

This new mission to the Gentiles needs a dynamic team. Barnabas travels all the way to Tarsus to find Saul, who was such a problem to the Jerusalem church. In Antioch there is room for him. Paul could not fit in at Damascus or in Jerusalem, but Barnabas is giving him a third chance.

> Now those who were scattered because of the persecution that took place over Stephen traveled as far as Phoenicia, Cyprus, and Antioch, and they spoke the word to no one except Jews. But among them were some men of Cyprus and Cyrene who, on coming to Antioch, spoke to the Hellenists also, proclaiming the Lord Jesus. The hand of the Lord was with them, and a great number became believers and turned to the Lord. News of this came to the ears of the church in Jerusalem, and they sent Barnabas to Antioch. When he came and saw the grace of God, he rejoiced, and he exhorted them all to remain faithful to the Lord with steadfast devotion; for he was a good man, full of the Holy Spirit and of faith. And a great many people were brought to the Lord. Then Barnabas went to Tarsus to look for Saul, and when he had found him, he brought him to Antioch. So it was that for an entire year they met with the church and taught a great many people, and it was in Antioch that the disciples were first called "Christians."

Acts 11: 19-26

From this dynamic Christian community in Antioch, not from the revered mother church in Jerusalem, the missionary journeys of Paul originated. The community at Antioch, inspired by the Holy Spirit, sent Barnabas and Saul on the first missionary journey, which would bring them to Cyprus and parts of what is now Turkey. They were accompanied by Mark, a cousin of Barnabas, in Cyprus. It would later develop that he did not have courage for the entire trip (Acts 13:13–14). At the point when Mark left, Luke begins to refer to Saul as "Paul" and indicates that he has emerged as leader of the mission, a big change of position from what the Christians of Antioch had anticipated.

> Now in the church at Antioch there were prophets and teachers: Barnabas, Simeon who was called Niger, Lucius of Cyrene, Manean a member of the court of Herod the ruler, and Saul. While they were worshiping the Lord and fasting, the Holy Spirit said, "Set apart for me Barnabas and Saul for the work to which I have called them." Then after fasting and praying they laid their hands on them and sent them off.

Acts 13:1-3

The Arrest of Peter

Back in Jerusalem, the persecution is continued by Herod Agrippa I, a grandson of Herod the Great who tried to kill the infant Jesus. James, the brother of John, is martyred. Then at Passover time, the time of Unleavened Bread (the same time as Jesus' Passion), Peter is arrested. He is kept under careful guard, but Herod does not know about the power stronger than his guard: the church is praying for Peter.

An angel appears in the prison cell and tries to wake Peter. Clearly, he is only partly successful. Luke paints a humorous picture of the angel with difficulty getting sleepy Peter out of bed, into his clothes, and out of the prison. Only when the angel leaves does Peter wake up to what is happening. Perhaps then he remembers that this is not the first time that an angel has rescued him from prison (Acts 5:17-26).

About that time King Herod laid violent hands upon some who belonged to the church. He had James, the brother of John, killed with the sword. After he saw that it pleased the Jews, he proceeded to arrest Peter also. (This was during the festival of Unleavened Bread.) When he had seized him, he put him in prison and handed him over to four squads of soldiers to guard him, intending to bring him out to the people after the Passover. While Peter was kept in prison, the church prayed fervently to God for him.

The very night before Herod was going to bring him out, Peter, bound with two chains, was sleeping between two soldiers, while guards in front of the door were keeping watch over the prison. Suddenly an angel of the Lord appeared and a light shone in the cell. He tapped Peter on the side and woke him, saying, "Get up quickly." And the chains fell off his wrists. The angel said to him, "Fasten your belt and put on your sandals." He did so. Then he said to him, "Wrap your cloak around you and follow me." Peter went out and followed him; he did not realize that what was happening with the angel's help was real; he thought he was seeing a vision. After they had passed the first and the second guard, they came before the iron gate leading into the city. It opened for them of its own accord, and they went outside and walked along a lane, when suddenly the angel left him. Then Peter came to himself and said, "Now I am sure that the Lord has sent his angel and rescued me from the hands of Herod and from all that the Jewish people were expecting."

Acts 12:1-11

In the same humorous tone Luke tells about Peter's return to the community gathered at the home of Mary the mother of

Mark, which has been praying for his release. When he knocks at the gate, Rhoda, the servant girl who answers the door, is so astonished she forgets to open the gate. When she reports to the others that he is there, they dismiss the idea as ridiculous, while he continues to wait outside in the cold. We can be like them, not really believing that God will answer our prayers. Prayer is more powerful than we realize!

After telling the community about his miraculous release, Peter leaves the Jerusalem area. The main part of his work is now done, and he is moving away from center stage, which will soon be occupied by Saul. He has the wisdom, which we all need, to know when to retire to the sidelines and make room for other actors.

> As soon as he realized this, he went to the house of Mary, the mother of John whose other name was Mark, where many had gathered and were praying. When he knocked at the outer gate, a maid named Rhoda came to answer. On recognizing Peter's voice, she was so overjoyed that, instead of opening the gate, she ran in and announced that Peter was standing at the gate. They said to her, "You are out of your mind!" But she insisted that it was so. They said, "It is his angel." Meanwhile Peter continued knocking; and when they opened the gate, they saw him and were amazed. He motioned to them with his hand to be silent, and described for them how the Lord had brought him out of the prison. And he added, "Tell this to James and to the believers." Then he left and went to another place.

Acts 12:12-17

Questions for Reflection

1. Peter was changed by bringing Gentiles into the home where he was staying and by accepting hospitality from a Gentile. Have you ever been changed because you

accepted a stranger into your home or accepted hospitality from a stranger?

2. Is there some kind of person or thing you were taught from childhood to avoid or look down on, but later learned to respect, as Peter had looked down on Gentiles but learned to respect them?

3. When have you found, as Peter did in his vision, that something you have always believed to be God's law was in fact not God's will?

4. The Jewish Christians were surprised when the gift of the Spirit was given to Gentiles. When have you been surprised at the person to whom God gave some gift?

5. Do you know of laypeople today who spread the faith as Christians who fled from Jerusalem did?

6. Can you think of people who, like the Jerusalem community that prayed for Peter's release, were astounded when what they prayed for actually happened?

7. What might be the feelings of a person, like Peter, who has been the center of the action but must step back to let someone else step forward?

Suggestions for Further Reading
Acts 10–12; Luke 7:1–10

CHAPTER EIGHTEEN

The Council of Jerusalem

Internal Conflict

WHEN PERSECUTION BROKE OUT AGAINST the church in Jerusalem, those who fled also spontaneously spread the gospel. However, they spread some of their own prejudices with it. These were Jews who from childhood had observed the Jewish law, with all its complicated demands about food, sex, Sabbath observance and so forth. They loved this law, which gave them a sense that they were following the will of God in all the details of their daily life. Jesus also had observed this law, and it never occurred to them to cease their observance of it when they became followers of Jesus. Some of them taught the Jewish observances as part of the Christian package. They could not imagine a Christianity separate from the synagogue.

However, more liberal teachers, like Paul and Barnabas, had already brought Gentiles into the church without requiring that they take up the burden of the Jewish law. The two views clashed violently, leaving the Gentile converts unsure about whether they were real Christians or needed to begin observance of the Jewish law before they could be saved by Jesus. This is the great theological issue of the first-generation Christians. Are we saved by Jesus or by the law? Or do we need both?

This is also a little like the issue that missionaries of every generation face. I have visited a Catholic church in Jordan that looks exactly like a modernized Gothic church in any American parish of the last generation, even with a large sign advertising bingo. Missionaries tend to bring their own culture along with the gospel, so that converts

identify their new faith with many things which are actually American or European. Later on, conflict can arise
when some want to use more of their native culture, for
example, using rice cakes instead of wheat bread for
Eucharist. These can be painful and difficult issues now, as
they were for the first Christians.

The issue of whether Gentile converts should be
required to follow the Jewish law was hotly debated, and
the church at Antioch was unable to come to a conclusion
about it. So they decided to refer it to higher authority, the
mother church in Jerusalem. This church was led, as most
churches probably were, by a group of elders, mature people whose wisdom could guide the community. However,
it also included the apostles, who had a very special authority for the whole church given them by Jesus. The church
at Antioch sent a delegation to consult both the leadership
groups in Jerusalem, apostles and elders.

On the way the delegation passed through Phoenicia
and Samaria, what is now Lebanon and northern Israel.
Everywhere they reported the marvel that in Antioch and
in the churches in Cyprus and Asia Minor established by
Paul and Barnabas even Gentiles were entering the church.
It is typical of Luke to tell us with what joy this news was
received. He sees both the infancy of Jesus and the beginnings of the church as times especially filled with joy.

However, when they arrived in Jerusalem, some
Christians, who had formerly been Pharisees, disapproved
of what was going on in Antioch. They held rigidly to what
they had always been taught. No one can be part of our
community without being circumcised and observing the
full Jewish law. Converts, no matter how sincere, bring into
their new life as Christians convictions from their previous
life. Conversion is a lifelong process by which we gradually
let go of things we thought were God's will but are not so
in the way in which we thought. These former Pharisees
had not moved as far along in the conversion process as
Barnabas and Paul.

Then certain individuals came down from Judea and were teaching the brothers, "Unless you are circumcised according to the custom of Moses, you cannot be saved." And after Paul and Barnabas had no small dissension and debate with them, Paul and Barnabas and some of the others were appointed to go up to Jerusalem to discuss this question with the apostles and the elders. So they were sent on their way by the church, and as they passed through both Phoenicia and Samaria, they reported the conversion of the Gentiles, and brought great joy to all the believers. When they came to Jerusalem, they were welcomed by the church and the apostles and the elders, and they reported all that God had done with them. But some believers who belonged to the sect of the Pharisees stood up and said, "It is necessary for them to be circumcised and ordered to keep the law of Moses."

Acts 15:1-5

Conflict Resolution

The apostles and the elders met together to consider the problem. Like the bishops at the Second Vatican Council, they debated at great length. We do not have a record of all the discussion. But we have the words Peter spoke after listening to all of it. He reminded them that God had called him to preach to Cornelius and witness the marvelous work of the Spirit in that Gentile household. And he stated clearly the theological issue involved. Jews and Gentiles alike are to be saved by the grace given through Jesus. Observance of the law is not necessary to salvation.

Peter's role then, like that of wise older leaders today, was to serve the unity of the community. He did that by patiently listening to all points of view, by reminding the community of the Cornelius experience in its early days, and by a clear statement of the basic theological issue. Many a grandparent today is called on to do the same in a family squabble.

Peter's authority gained an audience for Barnabas and Paul, who now had the opportunity to tell their story in a formal setting. The community listened more deeply this time. We have to hear a new idea more than once to really absorb it.

Next, James, the leader of the Jerusalem church, rose to speak. He was highly respected because he was a relative of Jesus and also because of his zealous observance of the Jewish law. Sometimes God uses those most devoted to the old to support the new. His was not an argument from recent experience, like Peter's and Paul's. He argued from the old Scriptures, sacred to all Jews. In the old text he found a new meaning to fit the new situation.

He supported the position of Peter, but added some conditions based on Jewish law. The Book of Leviticus (Chapters 17 and 18) laid down some minimum regulations about food and sexuality which should be observed by Gentiles living in Jewish lands so that it would be possible for them to associate with Jews without causing ritual contamination. James asked that Gentile converts observe these. This ruling would soon pass out of use, but it was important at a time of conflict to show respect for differing views by compromise. We can learn from James that change should always be made as gently as possible, with consideration for the feelings of those who do not want the change.

The long and probably painful process of the Council of Jerusalem had led to consensus. The assembled body had freed the new generation of Gentile Christians to move ahead. It was not the role of the old church of Jerusalem to undertake the new mission to the Gentile world, but it *was* their role to open the door to Paul and his coworkers to pursue their mission without losing continuity with the mother church and with Jesus. It is often the role of the old to free the young to follow a new call.

The work of the Second Vatican Council had many similarities with the work of the Council of Jerusalem.

Differing views, conservative and liberal, caused conflict beneath the surface that threatened to prevent the forward movement of the church. A wise old pope gathered those of every opinion for long sessions of listening to each other. They were finally able to come to a consensus which enabled the church to move forward in new directions without losing its unity.

Peter appears here for the last time. Since the conversion of Cornelius he has moved out of center stage. He reappears to lend his support to the new movement at this crucial meeting, as retired persons sometimes do today. Now, as far as Luke's story is concerned, he has completed his work and can retire altogether.

> The apostles and the elders met together to consider this matter. After there had been much debate, Peter stood up and said to them, "My brothers, you know that in the early days God made a choice among you, that I should be the one through whom the Gentiles would hear the message of the good news and become believers. And God, who knows the human heart, testified to them by giving them the Holy Spirit, just as he did to us; and in cleansing their hearts by faith he has made no distinction between them and us. Now therefore why are you putting God to the test by placing on the neck of the disciples a yoke that neither our ancestors nor we have been able to bear? On the contrary, we believe that we will be saved through the grace of the Lord Jesus, just as they will."
>
> The whole assembly kept silence, and listened to Barnabas and Paul as they told of all the signs and wonders that God had done through them among the Gentiles. After they finished speaking, James replied, "My brothers, listen to me. Simeon has related how God first looked favorably on the Gentiles, to take from among them a people for his name. This agrees with the words of the prophets, as it is written,
>
>> 'After this I will return, and I will rebuild the
>> dwelling of David, which has fallen;

from its ruins I will rebuild it, and I will set it up,
so that all other peoples may seek the Lord—
even all the Gentiles over whom my name has been
called.
Thus says the Lord, who has been making these things
known from long ago.'
Therefore I have reached the decision that we should
not trouble those Gentiles who are turning to God, but we
should write to them to abstain only from things polluted
by idols and from fornication and from whatever has been
strangled and from blood...."

Acts 15:6-20

The Council Document

It was important that the new consensus be communicated
in a clear form. So the apostles and elders drafted a letter. It
was clearly aimed at restoring peace of mind to the Gentiles,
who had been troubled by unauthorized preachers who
wanted to lay the burden of the Jewish law on them. Along
with the document, they sent living witnesses from the
Council of Jerusalem: Judas and Silas. (Silas will later become
Paul's companion in his missionary work.)

The teaching of the letter begins in an unusual way: "It
has seemed good to the Holy Spirit and to us." Through all
the debate of the Council, the Holy Spirit had been the
invisible force that actually determined the outcome. The
Spirit works through many of the human processes of our
lives also.

Then the apostles and the elders, with the consent of the
whole church, decided to choose men from among their
members and to send them to Antioch with Paul and
Barnabas. They sent Judas called Barsabas, and Silas, leaders
among the brothers, with the following letter: "The brothers, both the apostles and the elders, to the believers of
Gentile origin in Antioch and Syria and Cilicia, greetings.
Since we have heard that certain persons who have gone

out from us, though with no instructions from us, have said things to disturb you and have unsettled your minds, we have decided unanimously to choose representatives and send them to you, along with our beloved Barnabas and Paul, who have risked their lives for the sake of our Lord Jesus Christ. We have therefore sent Judas and Silas, who themselves will tell you the same things by word of mouth. For it has seemed good to the Holy Spirit and to us to impose on you no further burden than these essentials: that you abstain from what has been sacrificed to idols and from blood and from what is strangled and from fornication. If you keep yourselves from these, you will do well. Farewell."

Acts 15:22-29

Report to the Home Church

The letter from the Jerusalem church was received by the Antioch church with as much joy as the news about many conversions at Antioch had been received by the other churches. The Jerusalem delegates, Judas and Silas, were welcomed warmly. They were prophets, which does not mean that they foretold the future, but that they had a gift for encouraging Christians in their faith. The church in Antioch continued to flourish.

So they were sent off and went down to Antioch. When they gathered the congregation together, they delivered the letter. When its members read it, they rejoiced at the exhortation. Judas and Silas, who were themselves prophets, said much to encourage and strengthen the believers. After they had been there for some time, they were sent off in peace by the believers to those who had sent them. But Paul and Barnabas remained in Antioch, and there, with many others, they taught and proclaimed the word of the Lord.

Acts 15:30-35

A Personality Conflict

Paul and Barnabas had been companions on their first missionary journey, in Antioch and at the Council of Jerusalem. Paul must have had a special love for Barnabas because it was only Barnabas's support that persuaded the Jerusalem Christians to accept their former persecutor, and it was Barnabas who came to Tarsus to bring him to the fruitful missionary venture at Antioch, the beginning of his effective ministry.

Now it is time for the second missionary journey, to visit the churches they have founded to guide and encourage them. Paul suggests the trip and Barnabas agrees, but Barnabas wants to bring his relative Mark along. Mark had come along on their first journey, but abandoned them (Acts 13:13). Barnabas wants to give him a second chance, but Paul is not willing. Faith does not change our personalities; Barnabas is still gentle and trusting, Paul still harsh and judgmental. The whole church had been able to come to a consensus on its great theological issue, but these two men could not come to an agreement on whether to allow Mark to come with them.

They parted, Barnabas and Mark going to Cyprus, Barnabas's home territory, and Paul going into what is now Turkey, his home territory. They had not forgotten the Lord's command to go out two by two (Luke 10:1), so Paul invited Silas to come with him. Silas was not only a prophet, but a leading member of the Jerusalem community. His decision to join Paul in the mission to the Gentiles linked Paul in a new way to the mother church in Jerusalem.

So the irreconcilable conflict between the two apostles doubled the number of missionaries. It also left a message of hope for church ministers of every generation plagued with personality conflicts!

> After some days Paul said to Barnabas, "Come, let us return and visit the believers in every city where we proclaimed the word of the Lord and see how they are doing."

Barnabas wanted to take with them John called Mark. But Paul decided not to take with them one who had deserted them in Pamphylia and had not accompanied them in the work. The disagreement became so sharp that they parted company; Barnabas took Mark with him and sailed away to Cyprus. But Paul chose Silas and set out, the believers commending him to the grace of the Lord. He went through Syria and Cilicia, strengthening the churches.

Acts 15:36-41

—⁓—

Questions for Reflection

1. What examples can you give of problems that had to be resolved by a church group through much discussion?

2. How do you think decisions should be made about issues that affect the church?

3. This chapter emphasizes how important it was for Christians to listen to the stories of other churches. Do you think that is important in the church today? When do you do it?

4. Jewish observances had to be dropped so Gentiles could become Christian. Are there things American Catholics of the older generation were taught as part of their religion which need to be dropped so the faith can be handed on to people of another generation or another culture?

5. Were the documents of Vatican II accepted as joyfully in your parish as the letter from the Council of Jerusalem was in Antioch?

6. Do you know of good people who could not work together, as Paul and Barnabas could not? What is the best way to handle such situations?

Suggestions for Further Reading
Acts 15; Galatians 1:1-10

CHAPTER NINETEEN

The Journeys of Paul

The Gospel Comes to Europe

ONCE THE STRUGGLE WITHIN THE CHURCH about accepting Gentiles without making them first become Jews by circumcision had been resolved, Paul could begin the journey that would lead him to the ends of the earth. It can happen today, too, that we have to resolve certain issues within the church before our missionary work can be fully effective.

Luke's Gospel showed Jesus often on the road. This second half of Acts shows Paul always traveling. The Galilean rabbi traveling by foot through a tiny portion of the Roman Empire *looked* very different from the sophisticated Hellenized Jew sailing around the Mediterranean world, but the same dynamism pushed both of them on. That same dynamism looks still different today as Christians spread the gospel on television and over the Internet.

Peter completed his work at the Council of Jerusalem. He now disappears from Acts to leave Paul as the central figure. In order to emphasize the continuity in the story, Luke will repeatedly show Paul doing the same things Peter and Jesus had done before.

Timothy Joins the Team

Paul and Silas begin Paul's second missionary journey by revisiting the young churches founded by Paul and Barnabas on their first missionary journey in what is now Turkey. Everywhere they proclaim the message of the Council of Jerusalem: Gentiles can enter the Church without being circumcised or observing the Jewish law. But their enthusiasm in proclaiming this freedom was balanced by a strange little incident.

In Lystra they met a young man in whom Paul recognized a vocation to the missionary life. His name was Timothy, and his mother was a devout Christian, no doubt thrilled at the thought of her son traveling with Paul and Silas. Timothy had not been circumcised because his father was a Gentile. This was a delicate situation. Many Jews would consider that Timothy's mother had failed in her duty to have her baby circumcised on the eighth day. This was just the sort of thing that could prejudice Jewish audiences against Timothy as a Christian missionary. Paul was vehement in his condemnation of the circumcision of Gentiles, yet he had Timothy circumcised before accepting him into the missionary team. Paul was too mature to stick by his principles in a rigid way that would hinder the spread of the gospel.

> Paul went on also to Derbe and to Lystra, where there was a disciple named Timothy, the son of a Jewish woman who was a believer; but his father was a Greek. He was well spoken of by the believers in Lystra and Iconium. Paul wanted Timothy to accompany him; and he took him and had him circumcised because of the Jews who were in those places, for they all knew that his father was a Greek. As they went from town to town, they delivered to them for observance the decisions that had been reached by the apostles and elders who were in Jerusalem. So the churches were strengthened in the faith and increased in numbers daily.

Acts 16:1-5

Doors Closed and a Door Opened

Revisiting the established churches was not the main thing in Paul's mind. He was eager to plant the gospel in new places.

But where? The Christians at Antioch had not sent them off with a pre-planned itinerary. Whichever direction they wanted to go, the Spirit told them "no." We do not know how the Spirit delivered the message—perhaps by an interior voice, perhaps by circumstances. Maybe they couldn't get reservations on the next flight. Somehow, God communicated to them that they were not to preach in the Roman provinces of Asia, Mysia or Bithynia. They had been traveling nearly a thousand miles when God finally told them where they were to go.

The message came in a dream. Sometimes God cannot get through to us until we let go of our thoughts in sleep. The dream was not of an angel but of an ordinary man, a man dressed in the distinctive costume of Macedonia, what we would call northern Greece. This Macedonian was calling for help. Sometimes it takes a special revelation from God for us to see that a person needs our help.

Notice that Luke tells us that *he* (Paul) saw the vision, but *we* sailed. This is the first time "we" appears in Acts. There will be several others. These probably indicate that at these points Luke joined the missionary team. It is also an invitation to us, the readers, to become more involved, to imagine ourselves setting sail with Paul on his first journey to Europe.

They went through the region of Phrygia and Galatia, having been forbidden by the Holy Spirit to speak the word in Asia. When they had come opposite Mysia, they attempted to go into Bithynia, but the Spirit of Jesus did not allow them; so, passing by Mysia, they went down to Troas. During the night Paul had a vision: there stood a man of Macedonia pleading with him and saying, "Come over to Macedonia and help us." When he had seen the vision, we immediately tried to cross over to Macedonia, being convinced that God had called us to proclaim the good news to them.

Acts 16:6-10

—⁓—

Lydia Welcomes the Gospel

Paul, Silas, Timothy and Luke took a ship across the Aegean Sea, landed at Neapolis, and walked on a good Roman road which can still be seen today to Philippi, an important city that would make a good starting point for the mission to Europe. One can visit the ruins of Philippi today.

Not finding a synagogue, they went to a place by the river where they had heard that Jews gathered for prayer. They found only a women's prayer group, led by Lydia, a prominent businesswoman involved in the sale of luxurious purple goods. She was a foreigner and a woman without a husband to protect her. Since it was rare for women to remain unmarried, she was probably divorced or widowed. She functioned as an independent woman, head of her household.

I have visited the spot by the river outside the ruins of Philippi where tradition says Paul baptized Lydia. It is a lovely spot, and a Greek Orthodox church has been built there especially for baptisms. It has no altar, but the baptismal font is in the center of the church and an icon of Lydia at the entrance. I saw a large Greek family coming out proudly holding a baby who had just been baptized at the same place as Lydia.

Lydia's home became the base for the mission in Philippi. It is the first Gentile home to have that honor. The church is moving further from its Jewish roots both geographically and in other ways.

Luke's Gospel told us that Jesus was followed by women who provided for him and his companions out of their means (Luke 8:1–3). In the same way, Lydia provides for Paul's missionary band.

> We set sail from Troas and took a straight course to Samothrace, the following day to Neapolis, and from there to Philippi, which is a leading city of the district of Macedonia and a Roman colony. We remained in this city for some days. On the sabbath day we went outside the

gate by the river, where we supposed there was a place of prayer; and we sat down and spoke to the women who had gathered there. A certain woman named Lydia, a worshiper of God, was listening to us; she was from the city of Thyatira and a dealer in purple cloth. The Lord opened her heart to listen eagerly to what was said by Paul. When she and her household were baptized, she urged us, saying, "If you have judged me to be faithful to the Lord, come and stay at my home." And she prevailed upon us.

Acts 16:11-15

A Slave Girl Is Freed from a Demon

The story now moves from a wealthy businesswoman to a slave girl. This poor woman was possessed by a demon who told fortunes through her. Her owner made a good business out of her humiliation. The demon recognized Paul, as the demon possessing the man in the synagogue at Capernaum recognized Jesus (Luke 4:33-35). Paul did not want this kind of publicity, and he felt sorry for the woman, so he freed her from the demon.

I wonder if she became a Christian. Luke does not tell us. He is more interested in showing us how the miracle disturbed the profitable business based on the slavery of a woman. Paul was seen to be bad for business. He was beaten and imprisoned because he had freed the slave girl.

One day, as we were going to the place of prayer, we met a slave-girl who had a spirit of divination and brought her owners a great deal of money by fortune-telling. While she followed Paul and us, she would cry out, "These men are slaves of the Most High God, who proclaim to you a way of salvation." She kept doing this for many days. But Paul, very much annoyed, turned and said to the spirit, "I order you in the name of Jesus Christ to come out of her." And it came out that very hour.

But when her owners saw that their hope of making money was gone, they seized Paul and Silas and dragged them into the marketplace before the authorities. When they had brought them before the magistrates, they said, "These men are disturbing our city; they are Jews and are advocating customs that are not lawful for us as Romans to adopt or observe." The crowd joined in attacking them, and the magistrates had them stripped of their clothing and ordered them to be beaten with rods. After they had given them a severe flogging, they threw them into prison and ordered the jailer to keep them securely. Following these instructions, he put them in the innermost cell and fastened their feet in the stocks.

Acts 16:16-24

A Jailer Is Converted

Prison did not dampen the spirits of Paul and Silas. At midnight they were singing hymns, no doubt to the astonishment of the other prisoners. Some civil rights activists in more recent times have followed their example.

Since Peter had been freed from prison by God (Acts 12:6-12), we expect the same to happen to Paul. Sure enough, an earthquake jolted the prison doors open. Herod had executed the guards who failed to keep Peter in prison, and Paul's jailer clearly expected the same fate. He was about to kill himself when Paul called out to assure him the prisoners had not escaped. Paul refused freedom because he was called to free his jailer.

Paul converted the jailer and his entire family. This reminds us of Cornelius and of Lydia. In each case, the entire family became Christian, and they joyfully provided hospitality to the apostle. They celebrated with a festive meal in the middle of the night.

About midnight Paul and Silas were praying and singing hymns to God, and the prisoners were listening to them. Suddenly there was an earthquake, so violent that the foundations of the prison were shaken; and immediately all the doors were opened and everyone's chains were unfastened. When the jailer woke up and saw the prison doors wide open, he drew his sword and was about to kill himself, since he supposed that the prisoners had escaped. But Paul shouted in a loud voice, "Do not harm yourself, for we are all here." The jailer called for lights, and rushing in, he fell down trembling before Paul and Silas. Then he brought them outside and said, "Sirs, what must I do to be saved?" They answered, "Believe on the Lord Jesus, and you will be saved, you and your household." They spoke the word of the Lord to him and to all who were in his house. At the same hour of the night he took them and washed their wounds; then he and his entire family were baptized without delay. He brought them up into the house and set food before them; and he and his entire household rejoiced that he had become a believer in God.

Acts 16:25-34

Departure from Philippi

Paul, who did not want to get his new convert in trouble, quietly returned to prison. But in the morning, when the magistrates tried to dismiss him quietly, his more assertive side surfaced, and he declared his Roman citizenship and demanded a public apology. Roman citizenship was a kind of trump card throughout the empire, somewhat as U.S. citizenship is in today's world. It entitled one to privileges denied the rest of society.

After receiving his apology, Paul returns to Lydia's house for a final visit, then moves on. Paul always seems to be the troublemaker. If he leaves, the Christians can continue their life in peace.

When morning came, the magistrates sent the police, saying, "Let those men go." And the jailer reported the message to Paul, saying, "The magistrates sent word to let you go; therefore come out now and go in peace." But Paul replied, "They have beaten us in public, uncondemned, men who are Roman citizens, and have thrown us into prison; and now are they going to discharge us in secret? Certainly not! Let them come and take us out themselves." The police reported these words to the magistrates, and they were afraid when they heard that they were Roman citizens; so they came and apologized to them. And they took them out and asked them to leave the city. After leaving the prison they went to Lydia's home; and when they had seen and encouraged the brothers and sisters there, they departed.

Acts 16:35-40

Questions for Reflection

1. With which of these characters can you identify most easily: Lydia, the slave girl, the jailer? Why?

2. When in your life have you tried one direction after another and found only closed doors?

3. Have you, or someone you know, had an experience like Paul's dream at Troas that challenged you to move in a new direction? Explain.

4. Do you know any single, widowed or divorced women who make significant contributions to the church today, as Lydia did in her day?

5. Paul gave an important role in the church to a successful single woman and freed a slave girl who was being used for profit by her owner. What is the church doing today to bring out the gifts of strong women and free oppressed women?

Suggestion for Further Reading
The Letter of Paul to the Philippians

CHAPTER TWENTY

Athens and Corinth: A Study in Contrasts

Athens

From Philippi, Paul traveled to Thessalonika and Berea, then on to Athens. Athens was unique among the cities of Paul's world. It was not of administrative or economic importance, but it was the center of classical Greek culture. Young men of the upper classes from throughout the Roman Empire were sent there for advanced education. Paul had received an education in Greek culture in his hometown, Tarsus, which was also something of a university town, but of much less prestige than Athens.

I imagine Paul as a tourist, excited by his first sight of Athens, carefully studying the great art works that surrounded him there. His reactions were mixed. He was both impressed by the cultural treasures and disgusted by the pagan worship with which they were intertwined.

Until now, Paul had preached mainly in synagogues, where he presented the Christian message in terms taken mostly from the Old Testament. In Athens he made the first great attempt to present the gospel in terms taken from popular Greek philosophy. The result was an extraordinarily beautiful speech. The declaration of Vatican II on the relation of the church to non-Christian religions begins with a quote from it, perhaps to remind us how basic this speech should be in our thinking about non-Christians. It shows that, just as the Jewish Scriptures could lead Jews to Jesus, so pagan philosophy could lead pagans to him. God is not far from any human being because "in him we live and move and have our being," as the infant before birth lives and moves and has its being in its mother's womb.

The reaction to Paul's powerful words is an anticlimax: "We will hear you again about this." The intellectual dabblers moved on to some other novelty. In fact, Athens is the first city Paul was not run out of. The sophisticated intellectuals were neither open to conversion nor interested enough to fight Paul. Paul's failure to get a church started at Athens must have been a humiliation for him, but it can be a comfort for us in our times of failure.

While Paul was waiting for them in Athens, he was deeply distressed to see that the city was full of idols. So he argued in the synagogue with the Jews and the devout persons, and also in the marketplace every day with those who happened to be there. Also some Epicurean and Stoic philosophers debated with him. Some said, "What does this babbler want to say?" Others said, "He seems to be a proclaimer of foreign divinities." (This was because he was telling the good news about Jesus and the resurrection.) So they took him and brought him to the Areopagus and asked him, "May we know what this new teaching is that you are presenting? It sounds rather strange to us, so we would like to know what it means." Now all the Athenians and the foreigners living there would spend their time in nothing but telling or hearing something new.

Then Paul stood in front of the Areopagus and said, "Athenians, I see how extremely religious you are in every way. For as I went through the city and looked carefully at the objects of your worship, I found among them an altar with the inscription, 'To an unknown god.' What therefore you worship as unknown, this I proclaim to you. The God who made the world and everything in it, he who is Lord of heaven and earth, does not live in shrines made by human hands, nor is he served by human hands, as though he needed anything, since he himself gives to all mortals life and breath and all things. From one ancestor he made all nations to inhabit the whole earth, and he allotted the times of their existence and the boundaries of the places where they would live, so that they would search for God and perhaps grope for him and find him—though indeed he is not far from each one of us. For 'In him we live and move and have our being'; as even some of your own poets have said, 'For we too are his offspring.' Since we are God's offspring, we ought not to think that the deity is like gold, or silver, or stone, an image formed by the art and imagination of mortals. While God has overlooked the times of human ignorance, now he commands all people everywhere to repent, because he has fixed a day on which he will have the world judged in righteousness by a man whom he has appointed, and of this he has given assurance to all by raising him from the dead."

When they heard of the resurrection of the dead, some scoffed; but others said, "We will hear you again about this." At that point Paul left them.

Acts 17:16-33

Corinth

From Athens, the cultural center, Paul moved on to Corinth, sin city. Corinth in Paul's day has been compared to San Francisco during the gold rush. It was a hub city for sea travel and made much of its income providing entertainment for sailors. It also hosted huge crowds during the Isthymian games, which might be compared to our Super Bowl.

Today, the Corinth Paul knew is in ruins. A pilgrim group to which I belonged celebrated Eucharist among the ruins, feeling our kinship with the lively Christian community Paul founded there. The Greek Orthodox celebrate Vespers there on February 13, the feast of Saints Aquila and Priscilla, whom Paul met in Corinth.

As usual, Paul preached first in the synagogue, but when he was rejected there he turned to the Gentiles. Pagan Corinth must have been a strange and frightening setting for someone used to the high moral tone of the Jewish community. God told him in a vision, "Do not be afraid...there are many in this city who are my people."

What a shocking message for a devout Jew, used to thinking of only Jews as God's people! Paul probably felt much as Peter did when he had the vision of the unclean animals being offered for his lunch (Acts 10:1–48). Paul stayed in Corinth eighteen months, a long time for him.

While in Corinth, Paul lived and worked with a Jewish couple who were to be an important part of the Christian mission: Priscilla and Aquila. They had just come from Rome, and their description of the Christian community at the center of the Roman Empire may have stirred up Paul's desire to go there. Priscilla and Aquila were not Paul's converts; they seem to have worked with him as equal members of the missionary team.

> After this Paul left Athens and went to Corinth. There he found a Jew named Aquila, a native of Pontus, who had recently come from Italy with his wife Priscilla, because Claudius had ordered all Jews to leave Rome. Paul went to see them, and, because he was of the same trade, he stayed with them, and they worked together—by trade they were tentmakers. Every sabbath he would argue in the synagogue and would try to convince Jews and Greeks.
>
> When Silas and Timothy arrived from Macedonia, Paul was occupied with proclaiming the word, testifying to the Jews that the Messiah was Jesus. When they opposed and reviled him, in protest he shook the dust from his clothes and said to them, "Your blood be on your own heads! I am innocent. From now on I will go to the Gentiles." Then he left the synagogue and went to the house of a man named Titius Justus, a worshiper of God; his house was next door to the synagogue. Crispus, the official of the synagogue, became a believer in the Lord, together with all his household; and many of the Corinthians who heard Paul became believers and were baptized. One night the Lord said to Paul in a vision, "Do not be afraid, but speak and do not be silent; for I am with you, and no one will lay a hand on you to harm you, for there are many in this city who are my people." He stayed there a year and six months, teaching the word of God among them.

But when Gallio was proconsul of Achaia, the Jews made a united attack on Paul and brought him before the tribunal. They said, "This man is persuading people to worship God in ways that are contrary to the law." Just as Paul was about to speak, Gallio said to the Jews, "If it were a matter of crime or serious villainy, I would be justified in accepting the complaint of you Jews; but since it is a matter of questions about words and names and your own law, see to it yourselves; I do not wish to be a judge of these matters." And he dismissed them from the tribunal. Then all of them seized Sosthenes, the official of the synagogue, and beat him in front of the tribunal. But Gallio paid no attention to any of these things.

Acts 18:1-17

Departure from Corinth

Paul's work in Corinth ended with his trial before Gallio. Gallio dismissed the charges brought against him by the Jews. Luke wants his readers, who are citizens of the Roman Empire, to see that Roman law and order is basically favorable to the church.

As at Philippi, being in trouble with the law seemed to be a sign that it was time for Paul to move on. In Corinth he left behind a lively Christian community that perhaps comforted him for his failure at Athens.

With his coworkers Priscilla and Aquila, Paul went to the seaport near Corinth, Cenchreae. There he cut off his hair, perhaps to mark the beginning of a period during which he was under a Nazirite vow. This kind of vow was a devotional practice described in Numbers 6:13-20. A Jewish man or woman could set aside a period of time as especially sacred by refraining from wine or contact with a corpse and cutting his or her hair. At the end of the time, they made a sacrifice in the temple and cut their hair and burned it as part of the sacrifice. Luke, who was not Jewish, may not have had a clear understanding of this ritual. (He seems to place the cutting of the hair at the beginning rather than the end of the observance.) But it is clear that he tells the story to emphasize that Paul was a devout Jew. In the same way, he emphasizes that the parents of Jesus fulfilled the Jewish rituals for him as an infant, though he seems to have confused the presentation of the child in the temple and the purification ritual of the mother (Luke 2:22-24).

Paul, Priscilla and Aquila sailed to Ephesus, one of the great cities of the Roman Empire. Paul left Priscilla and Aquila there. He himself preached briefly in the synagogue. He was urged to stay on but felt this was not the time for him to work seriously in Ephesus. He hurried on to pay his respects to the mother church in Jerusalem and to spend time in Antioch, the community that had sent him on his mission. Luke wants to show that Paul is not a lone ranger, but continues his relationship with the center of the Christian movement. After this was done, he began his third missionary journey, revisiting churches he had established.

> After staying there for a considerable time, Paul said farewell to the believers and sailed for Syria, accompanied by Priscilla and Aquila. At Cenchreae he had his hair cut, for he was under a vow. When they reached Ephesus, he left them there, but first he himself went into the synagogue and had a discussion with the Jews. When they asked him to stay longer, he declined; but on taking leave of them, he said, "I will return to you, if God wills." Then he set sail from Ephesus.
>
> When he had landed at Caesarea, he went up to Jerusalem, and greeted the church and went down to Antioch. After spending some time there he departed and went from place to place through the region of Galatia and Phrygia, strengthening all the disciples.

Acts 18:18-23

Apollos

Back in Ephesus, Priscilla and Aquila had to deal with an unusual problem. Apollos was an eloquent preacher, but his theological training was not all that could be desired. The missionary couple took him aside discreetly, and set him straight. He had the humility to accept the further truth they gave him, and he became an effective missionary. Not every brilliant preacher would be so open.

> Now there came to Ephesus a Jew named Apollos, a native of Alexandria. He was an eloquent man, well-versed in the Scriptures. He had been instructed in the Way of the Lord; and he spoke with burning enthusiasm and taught accurately the things concerning Jesus, though he knew only the baptism of John. He began to speak boldly in the synagogue; but when Priscilla and Aquila heard him, they took him aside and explained the Way of God to him more accurately. And when he wished to cross over to Achaia, the believers encouraged him and wrote to the disciples to welcome him. On his arrival he greatly helped those who through grace had become believers, for he powerfully refuted the Jews in public, showing by the Scriptures that the Messiah is Jesus.

Acts 18:24-28

Disciples of John the Baptist in Ephesus

Paul's third missionary journey eventually led him back to Ephesus, the capital of the Roman province of Asia. For two years, this was the base from which he preached throughout the province.

There he met others who, like Apollos, were followers of John the Baptist. It is interesting that twenty years after John's death he still had disciples in places as far from his homeland as Alexandria in Egypt and Ephesus in Asia.

These "Baptists" were a problem for the early church, and because of them Luke works hard at clarifying the relationship between John and Jesus, always emphasizing the superiority of Jesus and the role of John as precursor. The first chapters of his Gospel are carefully structured to show the parallelism between John and Jesus and the superiority of Jesus. Luke's efforts to affirm a charismatic religious leader in a way that does not diminish the unique role of Jesus have been continued throughout the ages by the church when problems have arisen regarding devotion to Mary and the saints.

When these disciples of John the Baptist accept the fuller truth Paul offers, another Pentecost experience occurs. It reminds us of the original Pentecost in Jerusalem, where all present were Jews, and that at the house of Cornelius, where all involved were Gentiles but living in Judea and deeply influenced by Judaism. This Pentecost in Ephesus is in a thoroughly Gentile part of the world and indicates that the Spirit will continue to come in every part of the world where the gospel is preached.

> While Apollos was in Corinth, Paul passed through the interior regions and came to Ephesus, where he found some disciples. He said to them, "Did you receive the Holy Spirit when you became believers?" They replied, "No, we have not even heard that there is a Holy Spirit." Then he said, "Into what then were you baptized?" They answered, "Into John's baptism." Paul said, "John baptized with the baptism of repentance, telling the people to believe in the one who was to come after him, that is, in Jesus." On hearing this, they were baptized in the name of the Lord Jesus. When Paul had laid his hands on them, the Holy Spirit came upon them, and they spoke in tongues and prophesied—altogether there were about twelve of them.
>
> *Acts 19:1-7*

Separation from the Synagogue

Paul's pattern is always to preach first in the synagogue. Everywhere he is rejected by the synagogue authorities and then goes to the Gentiles. Ephesus is the last example of this pattern, showing that no matter how much rejection he experiences, Paul never gives up on his own people.

> He entered the synagogue and for three months spoke out boldly, and argued persuasively about the kingdom of God. When some stubbornly refused to believe and spoke evil of the Way before the congregation, he left them, taking the disciples with him, and argued daily in the lecture hall of Tyrannus. This continued for two years, so that all the residents of Asia, both Jews and Greeks, heard the word of the Lord.

Acts 19:8-10

Questions for Reflection

1. What is your favorite part of Paul's address to the Athenians?

2. Can you think of an example in today's world of adapting the gospel message to a particular group as Paul adapted it to the Athenians?

3. When in your life have you felt as you imagine Paul felt in Athens?

4. The gospel found fertile ground in the ancient "sin city," Corinth. Do you notice anything similar in today's world?

5. What couples do you know in the church today who work together as Priscilla and Aquila did?

6. How do you think we should we relate to people like Apollos who are enthusiastic about Jesus but have an imperfect understanding of him? Can you give examples of such people?

Suggestions for Further Reading
1 Corinthians; 2 Corinthians

CHAPTER TWENTY-ONE

The Journey Outward and Inward

Competition

Ephesus was famous for its magicians, so it is not surprising that Paul came into conflict with them there. The sons of Sceva were trying to imitate the miracles Paul did. They actually used the name of Jesus in their magic. But using the name of Jesus without a real faith commitment can be dangerous.

God did extraordinary miracles through Paul, so that when the handkerchiefs or aprons that had touched his skin were brought to the sick, their diseases left them, and the evil spirits came out of them. Then some itinerant Jewish exorcists tried to use the name of the Lord Jesus over those who had evil spirits, saying, "I adjure you by the Jesus whom Paul proclaims." Seven sons of a Jewish high priest named Sceva were doing this. But the evil spirit said to them in reply, "Jesus I know, and Paul I know; but who are you?" Then the man with the evil spirit leaped on them, mastered them all, and so overpowered them that they fled out of the house naked and wounded. When this became known to all residents of Ephesus, both Jews and Greeks, everyone was awestruck; and the name of the Lord Jesus was praised. Also many of those who became believers confessed and disclosed their practices. A number of those who practiced magic collected their books and burned them publicly; when the value of these books was calculated, it was found to come to fifty thousand silver coins. So the word of the Lord grew mightily and prevailed.

Acts 19:11-20

—⁓—

Planning the Itinerary

When it was time to continue his journey, Paul planned to revisit the Philippians, the Beroeans and the Thessalonians in Macedonia and the Corinthians in Achaia. He felt compelled after those visits to go on to Rome. His premonition that Rome was his ultimate goal was true, but he would actually go there in a very different way than he had planned.

> Now after these things had been accomplished, Paul resolved in the Spirit to go through Macedonia and Achaia, and then to go on to Jerusalem. He said, "After I have gone there, I must also see Rome." So he sent two of his helpers, Timothy and Erastus, to Macedonia, while he himself stayed for some time longer in Asia.

> *Acts 19:21-22*

Riot in Ephesus

Before he began the next stage of his journey, the most dramatic event of his two years in Ephesus occurred. Luke tells the story with verve and humor.

To appreciate the story, we have to be aware that Ephesus was a bit like a pagan Lourdes. People came from all over the world to worship at the great temple of the goddess Artemis there. Much of the economy was built on the pilgrim trade.

In Ephesus, Paul was bad for business on a larger scale than when he exorcized the slave girl in Philippi. The silversmiths who produced religious art were afraid they might lose their jobs. Their fear was as real as that of workers today who support their families by producing armaments when they hear of peace movements. The silversmiths instigated a riot, which Luke describes with great insight into mob psychology.

Paul seems, as usual, to be the troublemaker. He would

have rushed into the center of the riot, but wiser Christians keep him hidden till the riot has run its course and is quieted by a helpful Roman official.

About that time no little disturbance broke out concerning the Way. A man named Demetrius, a silversmith who made silver shrines of Artemis, brought no little business to the artisans. These he gathered together, with the workers of the same trade, and said, "Men, you know that we get our wealth from this business. You also see and hear that not only in Ephesus but in almost the whole of Asia this Paul has persuaded and drawn away a considerable number of people by saying that gods made with hands are not gods. And there is danger not only that this trade of ours may come into disrepute but also that the temple of the great goddess Artemis will be scorned, and she will be deprived of her majesty that brought all Asia and the world to worship her."

When they heard this, they were enraged and shouted, "Great is Artemis of the Ephesians!" The city was filled with the confusion; and people rushed together to the theater, dragging with them Gaius and Aristarchus, Macedonians who were Paul's travel companions. Paul wished to go into the crowd, but the disciples would not let him; even some officials of the province of Asia, who were friendly to him, sent him a message urging him not to venture into the theater. Meanwhile, some were shouting one thing, some another; for the assembly was in confusion, and most of them did not know why they had come together. Some of the crowd gave instructions to Alexander, whom the Jews had pushed forward. And Alexander motioned for silence and tried to make a defense before the people. But when they recognized that he was a Jew, for about two hours all of them shouted in unison, "Great is Artemis of the Ephesians!" But when the town clerk had quieted the crowd, he said, "Citizens of Ephesus, who is there that does not know that the city of the Ephesians is the temple keeper of the great Artemis and of the statue that fell from heaven? Since these things cannot be denied, you ought to be quiet and do nothing rash. You have brought these men here who are neither temple robbers nor blasphemers of our goddess. If therefore Demetrius and the artisans with him have a complaint against anyone, the courts are open, and there are proconsuls; let them bring charges there against one another. If there is anything further you want to know, it must be settled in the regular assembly. For we are in danger of being charged with rioting today, since there is no cause that we can give to justify this commotion." When he had said this, he dismissed the assembly.

Acts 19:23-41

Troas: Turning Point

After the riot in Ephesus, Paul traveled on as he had planned. As soon as they had celebrated Passover, the Days of Unleavened Bread, he and his companions, including Luke, sailed from Philippi back to Troas, on their way to Jerusalem. Troas is the port where Paul had received the revelation that he was to evangelize Macedonia. Now it is the place of another turning point in the life of Paul. So far, he has been a fiery young man, full of energy, traveling ever further and further, establishing churches throughout what are now Turkey and Greece. Like Jesus during his public life, Paul has enjoyed a very successful ministry.

Now he is older and it is time for a more important journey: to Jerusalem, to his passion. The journey outward, the mission, has to be balanced now by a journey back to the center, which is both beginning and end. For Luke, Jerusalem is the symbol of the sacred center in each of our lives. This final journey occupies half of Luke's story of Paul, just as the journey of Jesus to his Passion in Jerusalem occupies a large part of Luke's Gospel. Both Jesus and Paul seem possessed by a sense of the ultimate significance of this final stage of their journeys.

Sometimes we experience such turning points in our lives, when what we accomplish in the visible world becomes less important and our union with the suffering, death and resurrection of Jesus becomes foremost. This can happen, for instance, to one who receives the diagnosis of a terminal illness. For Luke, the Passion of Paul, in which he follows the footsteps of Jesus in his Passion, makes Paul a model for us more than his extraordinary missionary success did. It is in the last part of his life that he becomes most clearly a Christ figure.

It is significant that the Passion of Paul, like that of Jesus, begins around the time of Passover, and that it begins with a sort of preview of resurrection.

Luke tells the humorous story of young Eutychus, who sat on a windowsill listening to Paul. But when the sermon went on and on he fell asleep, fell out the window from the third story and was killed. Perhaps this is meant as a warning to preachers who do not know when to stop. Paul rushed downstairs, embraced the body of Eutychus as Jesus had taken the hand of the dead daughter of the synagogue official (Luke 8:54), and raised him from the dead.

[W]e sailed from Philippi after the days of Unleavened Bread, and in five days we joined them at Troas, where we stayed for seven days.

On the first day of the week, when we met to break bread, Paul was holding a discussion with them; since he intended to leave the next day, he continued speaking until midnight. There were many lamps in the room upstairs where we were meeting. A young man named Eutychus, who was sitting in the window, began to sink off into a deep sleep while Paul talked still longer. Overcome by sleep, he fell to the ground three floors below and was picked up dead. But Paul went down, and bending over him took him in his arms, and said, "Do not be alarmed, for his life is in him." Then Paul went upstairs, and after he had broken bread and eaten, he continued to converse with them until dawn; then he left. Meanwhile they had taken the boy away alive and were not a little comforted.

Acts 20:6-12

The Journey Continues

Perhaps Paul felt the need for some time alone or some exercise after the excitement at Troas. He chose to walk alone the twenty miles to Assos, the next port at which the ship docked. Luke then gives us what sounds like a traveler's diary. He is much more specific about the details of this final journey than of the missionary journeys, perhaps to highlight its importance. Paul felt such an urgency to get to Jerusalem for the feast of Pentecost that he did not even stop at Ephesus, where he had so many friends.

> We went ahead to the ship and set sail for Assos, intending to take Paul on board there; for he had made this arrangement, intending to go by land himself. When he met us in Assos, we took him on board and went to Mitylene. We sailed from there, and on the following day we arrived opposite Chios. The next day we touched at Samos, and the day after that we came to Miletus. For Paul had decided to sail past Ephesus, so that he might not have to spend time in Asia; he was eager to be in Jerusalem, if possible, on the day of Pentecost.

Acts 20:13-16

Farewell at Ephesus

The ship did stop at Miletus, a port not far from Ephesus. Paul invited the elders who led the community at Ephesus to meet him there. He gave them a farewell address which reminds us of Jesus' farewell address as given in Luke's Gospel (Luke 22:14-38). Paul feels the Spirit almost forcing him toward the climax of his life which must take place in Jerusalem. There have been Jews throughout the centuries who felt this compulsion to end their lives in Jerusalem.

From Miletus Paul sent a message to Ephesus, asking the elders of the church to meet him. When they came to him, he said to them:

"You yourselves know how I lived among you the entire time from the first day that I set foot in Asia, serving the Lord with all humility and with tears, enduring the trials that came to me through the plots of the Jews. I did not shrink from doing anything helpful, proclaiming the message to you and teaching you publicly and from house to house, as I testified to both Jews and Greeks about repentance toward God and faith toward our Lord Jesus. And now, as a captive to the Spirit, I am on my way to Jerusalem, not knowing what will happen to me there, except that the Holy Spirit testifies to me in every city that imprisonment and persecutions are waiting for me. But I do not count my life of any value to myself, if only I may finish my course and the ministry that I received from the Lord Jesus, to testify to the good news of God's grace.

Acts 20:17-24

The Parting

Farewells are an important part of life. There is a need to review the relationship, clarify issues that might be problems and also to look toward what is ahead for both parties as paths separate. Above all, there is a need to pray together and to give expression to the love that will continue after separation. Paul challenges us to think about the farewells in our lives.

And now I know that none of you, among whom I have gone about proclaiming the kingdom, will ever see my face again. Therefore I declare to you this day that I am not responsible for the blood of any of you, for I did not shrink from declaring to you the whole purpose of God. Keep watch over yourselves and over all the flock, of which the Holy Spirit has made you overseers, to shepherd the church of God that he obtained with the blood of his own Son. I know that after I have gone, savage wolves will come in among you, not sparing the flock. Some even from your own group will come distorting the truth in order to entice the disciples to follow them. Therefore be alert, remembering that for three years I did not cease night or day to warn everyone with tears. And now I commend you to God and to the message of his grace, a message that is able to build you up and to give you the inheritance among all who are sanctified. I coveted no one's silver or gold or clothing. You know for yourselves that I worked with my own hands to support myself and my companions. In all this I have given you an example that by such work we must support the weak, remembering the words of the Lord Jesus, for he himself said, 'It is more blessed to give than to receive.'

When he had finished speaking, he knelt down with them all and prayed. There was much weeping among them all; they embraced Paul and kissed him, grieving especially because of what he had said, that they would not see him again. Then they brought him to the ship.

Acts 20:25-38

A Visit to Tyre

On the way, Paul visited the Christians at Tyre. They had learned from the Spirit that disaster awaited him in Jerusalem and urged him not to continue the journey. But Paul was impelled toward Jerusalem and toward his passion, as Jesus had been.

When we had parted from them and set sail, we came by a straight course to Cos, and the next day to Rhodes, and from there to Patara. When we found a ship bound for Phoenicia, we went on board and set sail. We came in sight of Cyprus; and leaving it on our left, we sailed to Syria and landed at Tyre, because the ship was to unload its cargo there. We looked up the disciples and stayed there for seven days. Through the Spirit they told Paul not to go on to Jerusalem. When our days there were ended, we left and proceeded on our journey; and all of them, with wives and children, escorted us outside the city. There we knelt down on the beach and prayed and said farewell to one another. Then we went on board the ship, and they returned home.

Acts 21:1-6

—⁓—

Questions for Reflection

1. The Ephesians argued against Paul on religious grounds, but their real motive was economic. Where in the world today is religion a cover for other motives?

2. What businesses in today's world would suffer if the gospel was taken seriously, as the Ephesian silversmiths' business suffered?

3. Do you know any example in modern times of the kind of mob mentality seen in the riot in Ephesus?

4. Has there been a turning point in your life like Troas, where your journey shifted from a more active phase to a different pace or direction?

5. What significant farewell words of a parent or leader do you remember, either from your experience or from your reading?

6. If you were giving a farewell message to those you love, what would you want to include in it?

7. If you had been a member of one of the communities Paul visited on his journey to Jerusalem and heard the

prophecies that he would be arrested there, would you have tried to persuade him not to go? Why?

Suggestions for Further Reading

Luke 22; Acts 8 (Philip), 11:19–30 (Agabus)

CHAPTER TWENTY-TWO

Jerusalem

With Philip at Caesarea

At Caesarea, the home of Cornelius (Acts 10:1–48) and the seaport closest to Jerusalem, Paul's party stays with Philip, one of the seven who were appointed to help the apostles in the very first days of the church (Acts 6:5). It is he who baptized the Ethiopian eunuch. Philip had vivid memories of the young Saul on rampage trying to stamp out the infant church. But now he offers him hospitality on his journey toward Jerusalem. It is a special grace to experience reconciliation with old enemies toward the end of life.

Paul's Christian friends everywhere resisted the suffering toward which he was journeying, as Jesus did at the Mount of Olives. But, like Jesus, they came finally to say, "The Lord's will be done." Acceptance of the cross is usually not instant but a process beginning with a time of resistance.

When we had finished the voyage from Tyre, we arrived at Ptolemais; and we greeted the believers and stayed with them for one day. The next day we left and came to Caesarea; and we went into the house of Philip the evangelist, one of the seven, and stayed with him. He had four unmarried daughters who had the gift of prophecy. While we were staying there for several days, a prophet named Agabus came down from Judea. He came to us and took Paul's belt, bound his own feet and hands with it, and said, "Thus says the Holy Spirit, 'This is the way the Jews in Jerusalem will bind the man who owns this belt and will hand him over to the Gentiles.'" When we heard this, we and the people there urged him not to go up to Jerusalem. Then Paul answered, "What are you doing, weeping and breaking my heart? For I am ready not only to be bound but even to die in Jerusalem for the name of the Lord Jesus." Since he would not be persuaded, we remained silent except to say, "The Lord's will be done."

After these days we got ready and started to go up to Jerusalem. Some of the disciples from Caesarea also came along and brought us to the house of Mnason of Cyprus, an early disciple, with whom we were to stay.

Acts 21:7-16

Tension with the Jerusalem Christians

Paul was welcomed by the Christians in Jerusalem, but with reservations. The Council at Jerusalem had decreed that Gentiles who became Christian did not have to observe the Jewish law. But rumors in Jerusalem were that Paul was teaching that Jewish Christians were no longer bound by the law, which was quite a different thing. Paul may have taught that. The wise elders who led the Jerusalem community did not question him about his teaching. They simply suggested that he participate in a devotional practice which would reassure everyone that he was still a devout Jew. This was a Nazirite vow (Numbers 6:1-21). A person choosing to make this vow for a period of time did not cut his or her hair during that time. When the time was over the hair was cut and ritually burned in the temple. A rather expensive sacrifice was also required at this time, and Paul was asked to become a kind of sponsor for a group of Nazirites by paying for the sacrifice. Eventually Christians would abandon such Jewish practices as the Nazirite vow altogether, but this was still a time of transition when charity called for sensitivity to those who clung with intense devotion to the old ways.

When we arrived in Jerusalem, the brothers welcomed us warmly. The next day Paul went with us to visit James; and all the elders were present. After greeting them, he

related one by one the things that God had done among
the Gentiles through his ministry. When they heard it, they
praised God. Then they said to him, "You see, brother, how
many thousands of believers there are among the Jews, and
they are all zealous for the law. They have been told about
you that you teach all the Jews living among the Gentiles
to forsake Moses, and that you tell them not to circumcise
their children or observe the customs. What then is to be
done? They will certainly hear that you have come. So do
what we tell you. We have four men who are under a vow.
Join these men, go through the rite of purification with
them, and pay for the shaving of their heads. Thus all will
know that there is nothing in what they have been told
about you, but that you yourself observe and guard the law.
But as for the Gentiles who have become believers, we
have sent a letter with our judgment that they should
abstain from what has been sacrificed to idols and from
blood and from what is strangled and from fornication."
Then Paul took the men, and the next day, having purified
himself, he entered the temple with them, making public
the completion of the days of purification when the sacrifice would be made for each of them.

Acts 21:17-26

Riot in the Temple

The attempt at making peace backfired. While Paul was carrying out the ritual aimed at showing he was a good Jew, he was
seized by some of his enemies from areas where he had
preached and accused of teaching against the law of Moses
and, specifically, of defiling the temple by bringing Gentiles
into it. It seems that some Jews' devotion to the temple, which
should have been a good thing, was so fanatical it closed them
to the new message Jesus brought. Jesus, Stephen and Paul
were all condemned because they were seen as somehow
threats to the temple, that is, to the religious status quo.

Archeologists have discovered the signs that forbade Gentiles entrance into the main parts of the temple on pain of death. This charge that Paul had brought Gentiles into the temple was completely false, but it incited a riot that reminds us of the one at Ephesus. They dragged Paul out of the temple and shut the doors behind them so that the temple would not be defiled with blood. This was the culmination of all the times Paul had been put out of synagogues; he would never enter the temple again. He experienced rejection by his own people as Jesus had. The crowd kept shouting, "Away with him!" as the crowd had shouted about Jesus (Luke 23:18). As at Ephesus, it was the Roman authorities who intervened to save Paul. It is interesting that both the rioters in Ephesus and those in Jerusalem perpetrated their violence under the name of religion, though their religions were different.

As we approach the end of Paul's life, we learn more about his beginnings. Here we see both that he is still a citizen of Tarsus and that he is proud of his hometown. The Roman officer, who is bewildered by this commotion among the natives, is surprised, and perhaps a bit relieved, that the Jew he has rescued speaks good Greek.

When the seven days were almost completed, the Jews from Asia, who had seen him in the temple, stirred up the whole crowd. They seized him, shouting, "Fellow Israelites, help! This is the man who is teaching everyone everywhere against our people, our law, and this place; more than that, he has actually brought Greeks into the temple and has defiled this holy place." For they had previously seen Trophimus the Ephesian with him in the city, and they supposed that Paul had brought him into the temple. Then all the city was aroused, and the people rushed together. They seized Paul and dragged him out of the temple, and immediately the doors were shut. While they were trying to kill him, word came to the tribune of the cohort that all Jerusalem was in an uproar. Immediately he took soldiers and centurions and ran down to them. When they saw the tribune and the soldiers, they stopped beating Paul. Then the tribune came, arrested him, and ordered him to be bound with two chains; he inquired who he was and what he had done. Some in the crowd shouted one thing, some another; and as he could not learn the facts because of the uproar, he ordered him to be brought into the barracks. When Paul came to the steps, the violence of the mob was so great that he had to be carried by the soldiers. The crowd that followed kept shouting, "Away with him!"

Just as Paul was about to be brought into the barracks, he said to the tribune, "May I say something to you?" The tribune replied, "Do you know Greek? Then you are not the Egyptian who recently stirred up a revolt and led the four thousand assassins out into the wilderness?" Paul replied, "I am a Jew, from Tarsus in Cilicia, a citizen of an important city; I beg you, let me speak to the people." When he had given him permission, Paul stood on the steps and motioned to the people for silence.

Acts 21:27-40a

―⁓―

Paul Addresses the Rioters

Paul, the bilingual, bicultural man, shifts from Greek to Hebrew as he turns from the Roman official to the Jewish mob. Now he shows that he is also proud of the other half of his heritage. Though born in Gentile Tarsus, he was educated in Jerusalem by the famous rabbi Gamaliel. He was in his youth a fanatical Jew, a persecutor of Christians.

All this is to introduce his personal witness, the famous story of his conversion. Luke tells this story three times, an indication of its importance in his mind. The first time it was simply the account of the event (Acts 9:1-19). The second and third times, Paul in his mature years recalls the crucial event of his youth. Time can expand old memories. For the first time, we hear that the devout Jew Ananias had told Paul he was to give witness to all the world.

... [W]hen there was a great hush, he addressed them in the Hebrew language saying:

"Brothers and fathers, listen to the defense that I now make before you."

When they heard him addressing them in Hebrew, they became even more quiet. Then he said:

"I am a Jew, born in Tarsus in Cilicia, but brought up in this city at the feet of Gamaliel, educated strictly according to our ancestral law, being zealous for God, just as all of you are today. I persecuted this Way up to the point of death by binding both men and women and putting them in prison, as the high priest and the whole council of elders can testify about me. From them I also received letters to the brothers in Damascus, and I went there in order to bind those who were there and to bring them back to Jerusalem for punishment.

"While I was on my way and approaching Damascus, about noon a great light from heaven suddenly shone about me. I fell to the ground and heard a voice saying to me, 'Saul, Saul, why are you persecuting me?' I answered, 'Who are you, Lord?' Then he said to me, 'I am Jesus of Nazareth whom you are persecuting.' Now those who were with me saw the light but did not hear the voice of the one who was speaking to me. I asked, 'What am I to do, Lord?' The Lord said to me, 'Get up and go to Damascus; there you will be told everything that has been assigned to you to do.' Since I could not see because of the brightness of that light, those who were with me took my hand and led me to Damascus.

"A certain Ananias, who was a devout man according to the law and well spoken of by all the Jews living there, came to me; and standing beside me, he said, 'Brother Saul, regain your sight!' In that very hour I regained my sight and saw him. Then he said, 'The God of our ancestors has chosen you to know his will, to see the Righteous One and to hear his own voice; for you will be his witness to all the world of what you have seen and heard. And now why do you delay? Get up, be baptized, and have your sins washed away, calling on his name.'"

Acts 21:40-22:1-16

An Earlier Temple Event Remembered

As Paul continues speaking to the mob, we learn something else we had not known before. In the very temple he is accused of desecrating, Paul had prayed and been given a vision of Jesus telling him to leave Jerusalem and go to the Gentiles. As Paul remembers the vision of long ago, his part in the martyrdom of Stephen also comes back to his mind. As the end of life approaches, all kinds of memories come back.

> After I had returned to Jerusalem and while I was pray-ing in the temple, I fell into a trance and saw Jesus saying to me, "Hurry, and get out of Jerusalem quickly, because they will not accept your testimony about me." And I said, "Lord, they themselves know that in every synagogue I imprisoned and beat those who believed in you. And while the blood of your witness Stephen was shed, I myself was standing by, approving and keeping the coats of those who killed him." Then he said to me, "Go, for I will send you far away to the Gentiles."

Acts 22:17-21

The Riot Continues

The mob broke out into a riot again at the mention of preach-ing to the Gentiles. This reminds us of Jesus in the synagogue of Nazareth. The townspeople were favorably impressed by him at first, but when he mentioned God's interest in the Gentiles they interrupted him and violently threw him out of the city (Luke 4:16-40).

Again Paul was rescued by the bewildered Roman offi-cial, who then conceived the strange idea that whipping this troublesome Jew would make clear what was going on. As at Philippi, Paul proclaimed himself a citizen of Rome. Paul never speaks of the privilege of his Roman citizenship in his letters, but he does not hesitate to take advantage of it when he needs to in order to impress Roman officials.

> Up to this point they listened to him, but then they shouted, "Away with such a fellow from the earth! For he should not be allowed to live." And while they were shouting, throwing off their cloaks, and tossing dust into the air, the tribune directed that he was to be brought into the barracks, and ordered him to be examined by flogging, to find out the reason for this outcry against him. But when they had tied him up with thongs, Paul said to the centurion who was standing by, "Is it legal for you to flog a Roman citizen who is uncondemned?" When the centurion heard that, he went to the tribune and said to him, "What are you about to do? This man is a Roman citizen." The tribune came and asked Paul, "Tell me, are you a Roman citizen?" And he said, "Yes." The tribune answered, "It cost me a large sum of money to get my citizenship." Paul said, "But I was born a citizen." Immediately those who were about to examine him drew back from him; and the tribune also was afraid, for he realized that Paul was a Roman citizen and that he had bound him.

Acts 22:22-29

Questions for Reflection

1. Who in your life was not a friend at one time but became one later, as Phillip did for Paul? Was it hard to adjust to the change in the relationship?

2. Paul went through the rite of purification in order to show his enemies that he was a faithful Jew. Do you think this was a proper motive?

3. What do you think really led to the riot against Paul? Does anything similar happen in our world?

4. Luke shows Paul as having vivid memories of his childhood and youth as he approaches death. Have you ever seen this in anyone? Why do you think this happens?

5. Do you know anyone, like Paul, who was raised in two cultures? What advantages and disadvantages does this have?

6. What feelings do you imagine Paul having during the events in these readings?

Suggestion for Further Reading

Luke 23

CHAPTER TWENTY-THREE

Paul the Prisoner

Paul Before the Sanhedrin

Judea was not a popular assignment for Roman officials. The natives were notorious for their religious fanaticism and violent reactions to Roman administrative decisions. This tribune was making an honest effort to find out what had caused the riot in the temple. He called together the Sanhedrin, the Jewish council that governed in religious matters, and presented Paul to them. When Paul was illegally harassed during the trial, he was not as meek as Jesus had been during his trial.

Since he wanted to find out what Paul was being accused of by the Jews, the next day the tribune released him and ordered the chief priests and the entire council to meet. He brought Paul down and had him stand before them.

> While Paul was looking intently at the council he said, "Brothers, up to this day I have lived my life with a clear conscience before God." Then the high priest Ananias ordered those standing near him to strike him on the mouth. At this Paul said to him, "God will strike you, you whitewashed wall! Are you sitting here to judge me according to the law, and yet in violation of the law you order me to be struck?" Those standing nearby said, "Do you dare to insult God's high priest?" And Paul said, "I did not realize, brothers, that he was the high priest, for it is written, 'You shall not speak evil of a leader of your people.'"

> *Acts 23:1-5*

A Clever Maneuver and a Vision

Paul knew of the radical disagreements among Jewish religious leaders. The Pharisees, zealous laymen, believed in the resurrection of the dead and in angels. The Sadducees, the wealthy priestly class, believed in neither. Paul very cleverly distracted attention from the accusations against himself by claiming that he was on trial for his belief in resurrection, which precipitated such conflict within the Sanhedrin that the Roman soldiers had to rescue Paul again. The tribune was more puzzled than ever by the outlandish behavior of the Jews.

That night in prison Paul had a vision that laid out God's plan: he was to bear witness in Rome as he had in Jerusalem—as a prisoner.

When Paul noticed that some were Sadducees and others were Pharisees, he called out in the council, "Brothers, I am a Pharisee, a son of Pharisees. I am on trial concerning the hope of resurrection from the dead." When he said this, a dissension began between the Pharisees and the Sadducees, and the assembly was divided. (The Sadducees say there is no resurrection, or angel, or spirit; but the Pharisees acknowledge all three.) Then a great clamor arose, and certain scribes of the Pharisees' group stood up and contended, "We find nothing wrong with this man. What if a spirit or an angel has spoken to him?" When the dissension became violent, the tribune, fearing that they would tear Paul to pieces, ordered the soldiers to go down, take him by force, and bring him into the barracks.

That night the Lord stood near him and said, "Keep up your courage! For just as you have testified for me in Jerusalem, so you must bear witness also in Rome."

Acts 23:6-11

———

Paul Before Felix

The Roman official in Jerusalem found Paul's case too hot to handle, so he sent him to Caesarea, the capital, to the governor Felix.

Felix was fascinated by this strange prisoner, Paul, and liked to hear him talk. Felix took more than an ordinary interest in the Jews. He had even fallen in love with a Jewish woman, Drusilla, great-granddaughter of Herod the Great. He persuaded her to leave her husband and marry him, creating quite a scandal. When Paul spoke about righteousness and self-restraint, he hit a nerve, and Felix sent him back to his prison cell.

Felix knew Paul was innocent, but he kept him in prison in the hope of receiving a bribe. At the end of his term, even though he had lost hope of the bribe, he left Paul in prison in the hope of placating the Jews, who had complained to Rome about his corrupt government.

Paul probably could have raised money for the bribe that was expected. If he had, his life story would have taken a very different direction. The African Bible titles this section, "Gospel against Bribery."

At every level of these complex legal proceedings, the Roman officials seem uneasy, anxious about possible effects on their careers if they antagonize the Jews or if they violate the rights of a Roman citizen. The prisoner, in contrast, seems not at all anxious.

> Some days later when Felix came with his wife Drusilla, who was Jewish, he sent for Paul and heard him speak concerning faith in Christ Jesus. And as he discussed justice, self-control, and the coming judgement, Felix became frightened and said, "Go away for the present; when I have an opportunity, I will send for you." At the same time he hoped that money would be given him by Paul, and for that reason he used to send for him very often and converse with him.
>
> After two years had passed, Felix was succeeded by

Porcius Festus; and since he wanted to grant the Jews a favor, Felix left Paul in prison.

Acts 24:24-27

Festus Takes Over

The new governor, Festus, had to deal with this troublesome case left over by his predecessor. The Jewish leaders made many accusations against Paul but could not prove them, as they had not been able to prove the accusations against Jesus (Luke 23:10). Nevertheless, Festus suggested returning Paul to Jerusalem for trial. Paul knew that the Spirit was leading him, not back to Jerusalem, center of the narrow Jewish world, but forward to Rome, center of the Roman Empire. He used his privilege as a Roman citizen to appeal his case to the Emperor, Nero. The Spirit was moving the church toward the wider Roman world.

Three days after Festus had arrived in the province, he went up from Caesarea to Jerusalem where the chief priests and the leaders of the Jews gave him a report against Paul. They appealed to him and requested, as a favor to them against Paul, to have him transferred to Jerusalem. They were, in fact, planning an ambush to kill him along the way. Festus replied that Paul was being kept at Caesarea and that he himself intended to go there shortly. "So," he said, "let those of you who have the authority come down with me, and if there is anything wrong about the man, let them accuse him."

After he had stayed among them not more than eight or ten days, he went down to Caesarea; the next day he took his seat on the tribunal and ordered Paul to be brought. When he arrived, the Jews who had gone down from Jerusalem surrounded him, bringing many serious charges against him, which they could not prove. Paul said in his defense, "I have in no way committed an offense against the law of the Jews, or against the temple, or against the emperor." But Festus, wishing to do the Jews a favor, asked Paul, "Do you wish to go up to Jerusalem and be tried there before me on these charges?" Paul said, "I am appealing to the emperor's tribunal; this is where I should be tried. I have done no wrong to the Jews, as you very well know. Now if I am in the wrong and have committed something for which I deserve to die, I am not trying to escape death; but if there is nothing to their charges against me, no one can turn me over to them. I appeal to the emperor." Then Festus, after he had conferred with his council, replied, "You have appealed to the emperor; to the emperor you will go."

Acts 25:6-12

Agrippa Enters the Scene

The Jewish king, Agrippa, the son of the Herod who persecuted the church in Acts 12, and his sister Bernice came to visit Festus. Festus told them about the strange case of Paul. He confessed himself puzzled about how to explain the case to the emperor.

Like Pilate with Jesus, the Roman official Festus was glad to refer the bothersome case to a native king. (Only Luke tells us that Pilate sent Jesus to Herod during the Passion [Luke 23:6-12]. The incident, which did not seem important to other evangelists, is important to Luke because it shows the parallelism between Jesus' passion and Paul's.) Agrippa, like Herod at the trial of Jesus, was eager to hear this controversial prisoner for himself.

After several days had passed, King Agrippa and Bernice arrived at Caesarea to welcome Festus. Since they were staying there several days, Festus laid Paul's case before the king, saying, "There is a man here who was left in prison by

Felix. When I was in Jerusalem, the chief priests and the elders of the Jews informed me about him and asked for a sentence against him. I told them that it was not the custom of the Romans to hand over anyone before the accused had met the accusers face to face and had been given an opportunity to make a defense against the charge. So when they met here, I lost no time, but on the next day took my seat on the tribunal and ordered the man to be brought. When the accusers stood up, they did not charge him with any of the crimes that I was expecting. Instead they had certain points of disagreement with him about their own religion and about a certain Jesus, who had died, but whom Paul asserted to be alive. Since I was at a loss how to investigate these questions, I asked whether he wished to go to Jerusalem and be tried there on these charges. But when Paul had appealed to be kept in custody for the decision of his Imperial Majesty, I ordered him to be held until I could send him to the emperor." Agrippa said to Festus, "I would like to hear the man myself." "Tomorrow," he said, "you will hear him."

So on the next day Agrippa and Bernice came with great pomp, and they entered the audience hall with the military tribunes and the prominent men of the city. Then Festus gave the order and Paul was brought in. And Festus said, "King Agrippa and all here present with us, you see this man about whom the whole Jewish community petitioned me, both in Jerusalem and here, shouting that he ought not to live any longer. But I found that he had done nothing deserving death; and when he appealed to his Imperial Majesty, I decided to send him. But I have nothing definite to write to our sovereign about him. Therefore I have brought him before all of you, and especially before you, King Agrippa, so that, after we have examined him, I may have something to write—for it seems to me unreasonable to send a prisoner without indicating the charges against him."

Acts 25:13-27

Paul Tells His Story

Now we come to the climax of the many trials of Paul. Here he delivers his most eloquent speech and gives the fullest account of his conversion experience. Perhaps only at this last stage of his life was its meaning fully clear to him. Many elders looking back on their wedding day or conversion have a similar experience. The event of long ago glows with a new light because of the unfolding of its meaning over the years. He also shows that as his life approaches its end, he still has a vivid memory of the sins of his youth.

The theme of resurrection is important in this speech. It is as an innocent victim, already imprisoned for two years and facing the possibility of a death sentence, that Paul gives his most effective witness to the Resurrection. It has the special kind of power the Christian witness of the terminally ill and dying always has.

Agrippa said to Paul, "You have permission to speak for yourself." Then Paul stretched out his hand and began to defend himself:

> I consider myself fortunate that it is before you, King Agrippa, I am to make my defense today against all the accusations of the Jews, because you are especially familiar with all the customs and controversies of the Jews; therefore I beg of you to listen to me patiently.
>
> All the Jews know my way of life from my youth, a life spent from the beginning among my own people and in Jerusalem. They have known for a long time, if they are willing to testify, that I have belonged to the strictest sect of our religion and lived as a Pharisee. And now I stand here on trial on account of my hope in the promise made by God to our ancestors, a promise that our twelve tribes hope to attain, as they earnestly worship day and night. It is for this hope, your Excellency, that I am accused by Jews! Why is it thought incredible by any of you that God raises the dead?
>
> Indeed, I myself was convinced that I ought to do many things against the name of Jesus of Nazareth. And that is

what I did in Jerusalem; with authority received from the chief priests, I not only locked up many of the saints in prison, but I also cast my vote against them when they were being condemned to death. By punishing them often in all the synagogues I tried to force them to blaspheme; and since I was so furiously enraged at them, I pursued them even to foreign cities.

With this in mind, I was traveling to Damascus with the authority and commission of the chief priests, when at midday along the road, your Excellency, I saw a light from heaven, brighter than the sun, shining around me and my companions. When we had all fallen to the ground, I heard a voice saying to me in the Hebrew language, "Saul, Saul, why are you persecuting me? It hurts you to kick against the goads." I asked, "Who are you, Lord?" The Lord answered, "I am Jesus whom you are persecuting. But get up and stand on your feet; for I have appeared to you for this purpose, to appoint you to serve and testify to the things in which you have seen me and to those in which I will appear to you. I will rescue you from your people and from the Gentiles—to whom I am sending you to open their eyes so that they may turn from darkness to light and from the power of Satan to God, so that they may receive forgiveness of sins and a place among those who are sanctified by faith in me."

After that, King Agrippa, I was not disobedient to the heavenly vision, but declared first to those in Damascus, then in Jerusalem and throughout the countryside of Judea, and also to the Gentiles, that they should repent and turn to God and do deeds consistent with repentance. For this reason the Jews seized me in the temple and tried to kill me. To this day I have had help from God, and so I stand here, testifying to both small and great, saying nothing but what the prophets and Moses said would take place: that the Messiah must suffer, and that, by being the first to rise from the dead, he would proclaim light both to our people and to the Gentiles.

Acts 26:1-23

Questions for Reflection

1. Do you think Paul was right in refusing to give a bribe to Felix? Why? Do you know of similar situations today?

2. Why do you think Paul decided to appeal to the emperor? Do you think it was a wise decision?

3. Paul gave witness to Christ's Resurrection while he was a prisoner. Whom do you know who gave witness to belief in Resurrection while themselves suffering?

4. Do you have a conversion story or other significant event you feel the need to return to at key moments in your life, as Paul did? Do you feel you understand that event better now than you did when it happened?

5. Paul was an innocent victim of the complicated Roman legal system. Do you know of anyone who is a victim of a legal system today?

Suggestion for Further Reading

Galatians 1

CHAPTER TWENTY-FOUR

The End of the Journey

The Voyage Begins

Festus sent Paul to Rome because of Paul's appeal to the emperor. "We" appears again, making us aware that Luke joins Paul once more. This final voyage clearly impressed him deeply, as he describes it in more detail than any other.

> When it was decided that we were to sail for Italy, they transferred Paul and some other prisoners to a centurion of the Augustan Cohort, named Julius. Embarking on a ship of Adramyttium that was about to set sail to the ports along the coast of Asia, we put to sea, accompanied by Aristarchus, a Macedonian from Thessalonica. The next day we put in at Sidon; and Julius treated Paul kindly, and allowed him to go to his friends to be cared for. Putting out to sea from there, we sailed under the lee of Cyprus, because the winds were against us. After we had sailed across the sea that is off Cilicia and Pamphylia, we came to Myra in Lycia.

Acts 27:1-5

A Difficult Decision

At Myra (a port later to be famous as the home of Saint Nicholas) they found one of the many ships that sailed from Alexandria in Egypt to bring grain to Italy. This was the season of "the Fast," the Day of Atonement, which falls in September or October, just the time when the Mediterranean becomes too dangerous to travel. Paul, who had sailed often and experienced three shipwrecks before (1 Corinthians

11:25), saw that this trip was foolhardy, but those in charge paid no attention to the advice of the prisoner. So they continued their journey.

There the centurion found an Alexandrian ship bound for Italy and put us on board. We sailed slowly for a number of days and arrived with difficulty off Cnidus, and as the wind was against us, we sailed under the lee of Crete off Salmone. Sailing past it with difficulty, we came to a place called Fair Havens, near the city of Lasea.

Since much time had been lost and sailing was now dangerous, because even the Fast had now gone by, Paul advised them, saying, Sirs, I can see that the voyage will be with danger and much heavy loss, not only of the cargo and the ship, but also of our lives." But the centurion paid more attention to the pilot and to the owner of the ship than to what Paul said. Since the harbor was not suitable for spending the winter, the majority was in favor of putting to sea from there, on the chance that somehow they could reach Phoenix, where they could spend the winter. It was a harbor of Crete, facing southwest and northwest. When a moderate south wind began to blow, they thought they could achieve their purpose; so they weighed anchor and began to sail past Crete, close to the shore.

Acts 27:6-13

Storm at Sea

Luke, the literary artist, is at his best as he describes in precise detail the storm and shipwreck. Before they reached the port of Phoenix, a winter storm struck. After three terrible days of being buffeted by the storm, the passengers were in despair. Luke is too delicate to tell us how seasick they were.

Paul calmly eats and urges his companions to do the same. Nothing frightens him, because God has promised him he will give witness in Rome. His calm gives courage to his shipmates, and his good practical sense prevents the sailors from abandoning the ship.

But soon a violent wind, called the northeaster, rushed down from Crete. Since the ship was caught and could not be turned head-on into the wind, we gave way to it and were driven. By running under the lee of a small island called Cauda we were scarcely able to get the ship's boat under control. After hoisting it up they took measures to undergird the ship; then, fearing that they would run on the Syrtis, they lowered the sea anchor and so were driven. We were being pounded by the storm so violently that on the next day they began to throw the cargo overboard, and on the third day with their own hands they threw the ship's tackle overboard. When neither sun nor stars appeared for many days, and no small tempest raged, all hope of our being saved was at last abandoned.

Since they had been without food for a long time, Paul then stood up among them and said, "Men, you should have listened to me and not have set sail from Crete and thereby avoided this damage and loss. I urge you now to keep up your courage, for there will be no loss of life among you, but only of the ship. For last night there stood by me an angel of the God to whom I belong and whom I worship, and he said, 'Do not be afraid, Paul; you must stand before the emperor; and indeed, God has granted safety to all those who are sailing with you.' So keep up your courage, men, for I have faith in God that it will be exactly as I have been told. But we will have to run aground on some island."

When the fourteenth night had come, as we were drifting across the sea of Adria, about midnight the sailors suspected that they were nearing land. So they took soundings and found twenty fathoms; a little farther on they took soundings again and found fifteen fathoms. Fearing that we might run on the rocks, they let down four anchors from the stern and prayed for day to come. But when the sailors tried to escape from the ship and had lowered the boat into the sea, on the pretext of putting out anchors from the bow, Paul said to the centurion and the soldiers, "Unless these men stay in the ship, you cannot be saved." Then the soldiers cut away the ropes of the boat and set it adrift.

Just before daybreak, Paul urged all of them to take some food, saying, "Today is the fourteenth day that you have been in suspense and remaining without food, having eaten nothing. Therefore I urge you to take some food, for it will help you survive; for none of you will lose a hair from your heads." After he had said this, he took bread; and giving thanks to God in the presence of all, he broke it and began to eat. Then all of them were encouraged and took food for themselves. (We were in all two hundred seventy-six persons in the ship.) After they had satisfied their hunger, they lightened the ship by throwing the wheat into the sea.

In the morning they did not recognize the land, but they noticed a bay with a beach, on which they planned to run the ship ashore, if they could. So they cast off the anchors and left them in the sea. At the same time they loosened the ropes that tied the steering-oars; then hoisting the foresail to the wind, they made for the beach. But striking a reef, they ran the ship aground; the bow stuck and remained immovable, but the stern was being broken up by the force of the waves. The soldiers' plan was to kill the prisoners, so that none might swim away and escape; but the centurion, wishing to save Paul, kept them from carrying out their plan. He ordered those who could swim to jump overboard first and make for the land, and the rest to follow, some on planks and others on pieces of the ship. And so it was that all were brought safely to land.

Acts 27:14-44

—⁓—

Malta

The survivors of the shipwreck were warmly welcomed by the simple people of Malta. The leading man of the island provided hospitality for Paul and his companions. In return, Paul healed his father, as Jesus had healed Peter's mother-in-law (Luke 4:38,39). Astonished by the miracle, the natives brought all their sick and Paul healed them all, as Jesus had (Luke 4:40, etc.).

At this stage of his life, Paul is no longer a missionary. He makes no attempt to proclaim the gospel or establish a church. But he still has a ministry of healing, even during his passion. He is like Jesus, who paused in the turmoil of his arrest to heal the ear of the servant of the high priest which Peter had cut off (only in Luke 21:51). Christians ever since have felt called to the ministry of healing for the benefit of those of any religion or none.

The winter spent in Malta waiting for weather suitable for sailing was a peaceful interlude, a time of recuperation after the years in prison and the terrible shipwreck. God provided it before the climax toward which the whole of Acts has been moving: Paul's Christian witness in Rome.

After we had reached safety, we then learned that the island was called Malta. The natives showed us unusual kindness. Since it had begun to rain and was cold, they kindled a fire and welcomed all of us around it. Paul had gathered a bundle of brushwood and was putting it on the fire, when a viper, driven out by the heat, fastened itself on his hand. When the natives saw the creature hanging from his hand, they said to one another, "This man must be a murderer; though he has escaped from the sea, justice has not allowed him to live." He, however, shook off the creature into the fire and suffered no harm. They were expecting him to swell up or drop dead, but after they had waited a long time and saw that nothing unusual had happened to him, they changed their minds and began to say that he was a god.

Now in the neighborhood of that place were lands belonging to the leading man of the island, named Publius, who received us and entertained us hospitably for three days. It so happened that the father of Publius lay sick in bed with fever and dysentery. Paul visited him and cured him by praying and putting his hands on him. After this happened, the rest of the people on the island who had diseases also came and were cured. They bestowed many honors on us, and when we were about to sail, they put on board all the provisions we needed.

Acts 28:1-10

Italy

Paul and his companions were welcomed by the Christians of Puteoli (modern Pozzuoli), where they landed, and by the Christians of Rome. There had been a Christian community in Rome for twenty years before Paul arrived there. He knew of them from his friends Priscilla and Aquila, and had written them a long letter so that when he arrived he would not be a total stranger. When he wrote that letter, he had not expected that he would arrive accompanied by Roman guards!

Three months later we set sail on a ship that had wintered at the island, an Alexandrian ship with the Twin Brothers as its figurehead. We put in at Syracuse and stayed there for three days; then we weighed anchor and came to Rhegium. After one day there a south wind sprang up, and on the second day we came to Puteoli. There we found believers and were invited to stay with them for seven days. And so we came to Rome. The believers from there, when they heard of us, came as far as the Forum of Appius and Three Taverns to meet us. On seeing them, Paul thanked God and took courage.

When we came into Rome, Paul was allowed to live by himself, with the soldier who was guarding him.

Acts 28:11-16

Proclamation in Rome

In Rome, Paul made one last strenuous effort to convince his fellow-Jews of the gospel message. As has happened throughout the story, some believed, but the majority refused. So Acts ends with this final message: since the Jews have hardened their hearts, the salvation of God is offered to the Gentiles.

Three days later he called together the local leaders of the Jews. When they had assembled, he said to them, "Brothers, though I had done nothing against our people or the customs of our ancestors, yet I was arrested in Jerusalem and handed over to the Romans. When they had examined me, the Romans wanted to release me, because there was no reason for the death penalty in my case. But when the Jews objected, I was compelled to appeal to the emperor—even though I had no charge to bring against my nation. For this reason therefore I have asked to see you and speak with you, since it is for the sake of the hope of Israel that I am bound with this chain." They replied, "We have received no letters from Judea about you, and none of the brothers coming here has reported or spoken anything evil about you. But we would like to hear from you what you think, for with regard to this sect we know that everywhere it is spoken against."

After they had set a day to meet with him, they came to him at his lodgings in great numbers. From morning until evening he explained the matter to them, testifying to the kingdom of God and trying to convince them about Jesus both from the law of Moses and from the prophets. Some were convinced by what he had said, while others refused to believe. So they disagreed with each other; and as they were leaving, Paul made one further statement: "The Holy Spirit was right in saying to your ancestors through the prophet Isaiah,

'Go to this people and say,
You will indeed listen, but never understand,
    and you will indeed look, but never perceive.
For this people's heart has grown dull,
    and their ears are hard of hearing,
        and they have shut their eyes;

> so that they might not look with their eyes,
>   and listen with their ears,
> and understand with their heart and turn—
>   and I would heal them.'
> Let it be known to you then that this salvation of God
> has been sent to the Gentiles; they will listen."

Acts 28:17-28

Conclusion?

Acts seems to end in midair. We never learn what happened in the legal proceedings we have been following for so long. If Festus's letter was lost in the shipwreck, officials in Rome may have been even more puzzled about this prisoner than those in Judea had been. Luke does not tell us. Tradition tells us that Paul was eventually beheaded in Rome, but Luke does not say that either.

We need to look at the whole of Acts to see what Luke is trying to do. The first half of Acts centered on Peter, but after the Council of Jerusalem Peter simply disappears from the story. Nothing is said of his further preaching or his death. Luke is not writing a book about Peter, but one about the spread of the gospel.

In the same way, Luke makes no attempt to follow Paul to the end of his life. The story of Acts is in one sense complete, because the center of the church has shifted from Jerusalem to Rome. But the bigger story, the spread of the gospel, continues today and beyond. Perhaps the rather unsettling way Luke ends Acts is meant to jar us readers into awareness that the story continues in our lives.

> He lived there two whole years at his own expense and welcomed all who came to him, proclaiming the kingdom of God and teaching about the Lord Jesus Christ with all boldness and without hindrance.

Acts 28:30-31

Questions for Reflection

1. Have you ever had an experience that felt like a ship-wreck? Were there kind people like those of Malta to help you afterward?

2. Do you know of someone who, like Jesus and Paul, reached out to heal others even during their own time of suffering?

3. When have there been pauses for recuperation in your life, like Paul's months in Malta?

4. God's plan to bring Paul to Rome was carried out through corrupt politics. When have you experienced good coming out of evil?

5. Do you like the way Luke concludes Acts, or would you have preferred he stop sooner or continue on until the conclusion of Paul's case? Why?

Suggestions for Further Reading

The Letter to Philemon (Some scholars believe this was written during Paul's imprisonment in Caesarea or Rome); the Letter to the Romans

Key Places in the Acts of the Apostles

If you liked this book, try

Scott, Macrina, O.S.F. *Bible Stories Revisited: Discover Your Story in the Old Testament* (St. Anthony Messenger Press, 1999). Highlights of the Old Testament story with commentary and reflection questions in the same format as the present volume.

Other Books on the Bible

Brown, Raymond E. *Reading the Gospels with the Church from Christmas through Easter* (St. Anthony Messenger Press, 1996). An introduction to a Catholic approach to Scripture, with reflections on the Gospels for the principal parts of the church year. This is very simply put by an outstanding scholar.

The Denver Catholic Biblical School Program (Paulist Press). This is a serious four-volume study program covering every book of the Bible. It can be used in a group or alone, but requires substantial study time in either case.

Rohr, Richard, and Joseph Martos. *The Great Themes of Scripture: Old Testament* and *The Great Themes of Scripture: New Testament* (St. Anthony Messenger Press, 1987 and 1988). Classic introduction to the spiritual themes of the Bible.

Weber, Gerard P., and Robert Miller. *Breaking Open the Gospel of Matthew; Breaking Open the Gospel of Mark; Breaking Open the Gospel of Luke; Breaking Open the Gospel of John* (St. Anthony Messenger Press, 1998, 1994, 1990, 1995). These four volumes include discussion questions and are ideal for personal reflection on the Gospels or small group discussion.

Helps for the Study of the Gospel of Luke

Apicella, Raymond. *Journeys into Luke: 16 Lessons of Exploration and Discovery* (St. Anthony Messenger Press, 1992). A carefully designed workbook for an introductory study of Luke.

Himes, Michael. *The Vision of the Gospels: The Gospel of Luke* (St. Anthony Messenger Press). In this half-hour video, Father Himes presents an excellent lecture on the Gospel of Luke, stressing its emphasis on compassion. Even those already familiar with Luke will be surprised by some of his insights.

Johnson, Luke Timothy. *The Gospel of Luke* (Liturgical Press, 1991). A fine scholarly commentary.

Laverdiere, Eugene, s.s.s. *The Holy Spirit in Luke* (St. Anthony Messenger Press). These cassettes present two insightful talks on the Holy Spirit in the first chapters of the Gospel of Luke and the first chapters of Acts. Father Laverdiere combines outstanding scriptural scholarship with personal experience.

Reid, Barbara E., o.p. *A Retreat with Luke: Stepping Out on the Word of God* (St. Anthony Messenger Press, 2000). This book provides seven retreat sessions—each with opening story and prayer and presentation of a theme of Luke's Gospel in the form of a monologue by Luke, Jesus or some Gospel character. Questions for reflection and a closing prayer are also included for each session. Though written by a Scripture scholar, this book is addressed to the ordinary Christian seeking a deeper spiritual life.

———. *Women in the Gospel of Luke* (St. Anthony Messenger Press). In the three talks on these cassettes, Sister Barbara Reid wrestles with the problems posed by the Gospel of Luke, and the scripture generally, for a feminist.

Yanos, Susan. *Woman, You Are Free* (St. Anthony Messenger Press). This book uses the Gospel of Luke as a starting point for reflections on women's issues, especially the tension between service in the home and self-fulfillment. It provides guidance for personal reflection or for small groups of women willing to share deeply about their personal issues.

Books on the Spirituality of Aging

Fischer, Kathleen. *Winter Grace: Spirituality and Aging* (Upper Room Books, 1998). This classic was previously published by Paulist Press. If you are going to read only one book on the subject, read this.

Leder, Drew. *Spiritual Passages: Embracing Life's Sacred Journey* (Jeremy P. Tarcher/Putnam, 1997). This study of insights on aging from the great religious traditions of the world shows how much wisdom we all have to share.

McDonnell, s.s.n.d., Rea, and Rachel Callahan, c.s.c. *Harvest Us Home: Good News as We Age* (St. Anthony Messenger Press, 2000). These thought-provoking reflections on aging are all connected with the image of a garden.

Schachter-Shalomi, Zalman and Ronald S. Miller. *From Age-ing to Sage-ing: A Profound New Vision of Growing Older* (Warner Books, 1995). New and exciting insights on the challenge of eldering today. A groundbreaking book by a rabbi, suitable for Christians and Jews.

Tournier, Paul. *Learn to Grow Old.* (Westminster/John Knox Press, 1972). This classic was originally published under the title "Learning to Grow Old." Deep practical wisdom from a Christian psychotherapist.

Periodical

Scripture from Scratch (St. Anthony Messenger Press). An excellent four-page article each month, with suggestions for praying with Scripture, living the Scripture, discussing the Scripture. A painless way to continue to grow in your understanding of the Bible. Bulk rates are available; very suitable for group discussion. Back issues can be ordered separately, and *Luke's Gospel: Like Entering a Painting,* by Eugene LaVerdiere, s.s.s., is particularly good and would be suitable for distribution to an entire congregation at the beginning of the Year of Luke.